Christmas 1960

Ann
with Much Love:
Mother

The Saving Life of Christ

The
Saving Life of Christ

by

MAJOR W. IAN THOMAS, D.S.O., T.D.

ZONDERVAN PUBLISHING HOUSE
GRAND RAPIDS   MICHIGAN

This printing — 1963

Printed in the United States of America

MEET THE MAJOR

An Introduction* by Dr. V. Raymond Edman,
President, Wheaton College

SOME CHRISTIANS learn that the Lord can make life an adventure. Major W. Ian Thomas of England is one of them.

The major is every inch a soldier. With his infantry battalion he served in the British Expeditionary Forces in Belgium at the outset of World War II, and took part in the evacuation at Dunkirk. Often in combat, in France, Italy, Greece, and elsewhere during that long war, he found the Lord Jesus to be his complete sufficiency. The major is likewise a soldier of the cross, faithful to the Captain of our salvation. He has found life an adventure with God and for Him, a pageant of triumph in Christ.

Reared in a "respectable" middle class English home, he was taken to church and taught its precepts. He learned little or nothing of the Bible, however, either at home or in the church attended by the family. At the age of twelve he was invited to a Bible study group of the Crusaders' Union by a lad of thirteen who, during that year, had received Christ as his Saviour. The Bible began to be meaningful to young Ian, and the following summer, still twelve years old, he was converted to Christ at a Crusaders' Union camp. That decision was made when he was alone, and simply by praying earnestly, "Lord Jesus, please be my Saviour!"

At the age of fifteen, he felt convinced that he should devote all of his life to the service of the Lord Jesus. He told God that he would become a missionary. He began to preach,

*This Introduction was taken from a chapter in Dr. Edman's book, *They Found the Secret.*

5

out in the open air at Hampstead Heath, at that early age. He was also actively engaged in Sunday school work, as well as in the Crusaders' Bible class. Life began to be a round of ceaseless activity. . . .

Speaking of his youthful decision to become a missionary, he said: "I began to consider the best area in which I could become a missionary, and the best means I could employ to be most effective — perfectly sincere and genuine questions." The first missionary influence upon young Ian's life came through a doctor serving in Nigeria, in the Housa Band. "First impressions are often the strongest," related Major Thomas, and so it became his ambition one day to go and join the Housa Band in Nigeria, West Africa. He thought the best thing for him to do was to become a doctor. . . .

At the university Ian became a leader in the Inter-Varsity Fellowship group. If ever there was any evangelistic activity going on, this youthful zealot was "buzzing around the place, every holiday, every spare moment!" He started a slum club down in the East End of London. "Out of a sheer desire to win souls, to go out and get them, I was a windmill of activity until, at the age of nineteen, every moment of my day was packed tight with doing things . . ."

"Thus by the age of nineteen, I had been reduced to a state of complete exhaustion spiritually, until I felt that there was no point in going on. . . .

"Then, one night in November, that year, just at midnight . . . I got down on my knees before God, and I just wept in sheer despair. I said 'Oh, God, I know that I am saved. I love Jesus Christ. I am perfectly convinced that I am converted. With all my heart I have wanted to serve Thee. I have tried to my uttermost and I am a hopeless failure!' . . . That night things happened.

"I can honestly say that I had never once heard from the lips of men the message that came to me then. . . . but God, that night simply focused upon me the Bible message of *Christ Who is our Life*. . . . the Lord seemed to make plain to me that night, through my tears of bitterness: 'You see, for seven years, with utmost sincerity, you have been trying to live *for* Me, on My behalf, the life that I have been waiting for seven years to live *through* you."

That night, all in the space of an hour, Ian Thomas discovered the secret of the adventurous life. He said:

"I got up the next morning to an entirely different Christian life, but I want to emphasize this: I had not received one iota more than I had already had for seven years! . . ."

Thus step by step the Most High led His trusting and obedient servant into paths that he neither foresaw nor chose, but they were pathways of service eminently satisfying and always adventurous. Instead of medical school and the mission field, the ministry was evangelism throughout Britain, especially among young people. Before World War II broke out, he had six wonderful years of ever-expanding ministry in sharing the secret of the life that is Christ.

"I found that it is anything but inactivity (standing back and saying, 'I thank Thee, Lord, this is Thy situation!'). Since the war alone I have traveled a quarter of a million miles, 45,000 this year. . . . It has been my joy to preach in Norway, and Denmark, in Germany, Austria, Switzerland, the United States and Canada, apart from the British Isles, . . . It is not inactivity, it is simply His activity, and that is what makes the difference."

FOREWORD

I have known the author of this book for many years. He and I have been closely associated from time to time in the ministry of the Word of God and I have often received personal blessing in my own life through his ministry.

I am sure that the emphasis of this book is something that is urgently needed in this country today and indeed in every area where the message of saving faith in Christ is made known. To so many people, the Lord is in danger of being no more than a patron of our systematic theology instead of the Christ Who is our life. There is such a tendency to departmentalize Christian living and to regard our devotions as one department and then to live for the rest of our time almost as religious pagans.

This book strikes home at that attitude and presents to us the triumphant life of our risen Lord indwelling us by His Spirit as the one vital essential for Christian living.

It will be my earnest prayer that this book receives the attention and interest that it deserves and that its message may be a rich blessing to many thousands of readers.

—Alan Redpath

CONTENTS

Introduction by Dr. V. Raymond Edman

Foreword by Rev. Alan Redpath

The Saving Life of Christ

1

The Saving Life of Christ

THERE IS SOMETHING WHICH MAKES CHRISTIANITY MORE THAN a religion, more than an ethic, and more than the idle dream of the sentimental idealist. It is this something which makes it relevant to each one of us right now as a contemporary experience. It is the fact that Christ *Himself* is the very life content of the Christian faith. It is He who makes it "tick." "Faithful is he that calleth you, who also will do it" (I Thessalonians 5:24). The One who calls you is the One who does that to which He calls you. "For it is God which worketh in you, both to will and to do of His good pleasure" (Philippians 2:13). He is Himself the very dynamic of all His demands.

Christ did not die simply that you might be saved from a bad conscience, or even to remove the stain of past failure, but to "clear the decks" for divine action. You have been told that Christ died to save you. This is gloriously true in a very limited, though vital sense. In Romans 5:10 we read, "If, when we were enemies, we were reconciled to God by the death of his Son, much more, being reconciled, we shall be saved by his life." The Lord Jesus Christ therefore ministers to you in two distinct ways — He reconciles you to God by His death, and He saves you by His life.

I would like to examine with you what this implies. The very first word of the Gospel is a word of reconciliation, so that "we are ambassadors for Christ, as though God did beseech you by us; we pray you in Christ's stead, be ye reconciled to God" (II Corinthians 5:20). This is a call to the sinner to be at peace with God Himself. How is this possible? Only by virtue of the fact that "God was in Christ, reconciling the world unto Himself" (II Corinthians 5:19).

13

God in righteousness has no option but to find you guilty as a sinner and to pass upon you the sentence of death, the forfeiture of His Holy Spirit, and alienation from the life of God — by nature dead in trespasses and sins. But more than nineteen hundred years ago, God in Christ stepped out of eternity into time, and there are extended to you today the nail-pierced hands of One who suffered, "the just for the unjust," to bring you back to God (I Peter 3:18). "He bare our sins in his own body on the tree" (I Peter 2:24).

This is what makes the Gospel at once so urgent! Mental assent is not enough — a moral choice is imperative! Christ is God's last word to man and God's last word to you, and He demands an answer.

Your response to Jesus Christ will determine your condition in the sight of God — redeemed or condemned!

This, however, is but the beginning of the story, "for if, when we were enemies, we were reconciled to God by the death of his Son, much more, being reconciled, [*now an accomplished fact,*] we shall be saved [*as a continuing process*] by His life" (Romans 5:10). The glorious fact of the matter is this — no sooner has God reconciled to Himself the man who has responded to His call, than He re-imparts to him, as a forgiven sinner, the presence of the Holy Spirit, and this restoration to him of the Holy Spirit constitutes what the Bible calls regeneration, or new birth. Titus 3:5 and 6, — "Not by works of righteousness which we have done, but according to his mercy he saved us, by the washing of regeneration, and the renewing of the Holy Ghost; which he shed on us abundantly through Jesus Christ our Saviour."

On the third morning after His crucifixion, the Lord Jesus Christ rose from the dead and appeared to His disciples. He instructed them for some forty days and then ascended to the Father. On the first day of Pentecost He returned, not this time to be *with them* externally — clothed with that sinless humanity that God had prepared for Him, being conceived of the Holy Spirit in the womb of Mary — but now to be *in them,* imparting *to them* His own divine nature, clothing Himself with *their* humanity, so that they each became "members in particular" of a new, corporate body through which Christ expressed Himself to the world of their day. He spoke with their lips. He worked with their hands. This was the miracle of new birth, and this remains the very heart of the Gospel!

"Faithful is he that calleth you, who also will *do it.*" The One who calls you to a life of righteousness is the One who by your consent lives that life of righteousness *through* you! The One who calls you to minister to the needs of humanity is the One who by your consent ministers to the needs of humanity *through* you! The One who calls you to go into all the world and preach the Gospel to every creature, is the One who by your consent, goes into all the world and preaches the Gospel to every creature *through* you!

This is the divine genius that saves a man from the futility of self-effort. It relieves the Christian of the burden of trying to pull himself up by his own bootstraps! If it were not for this divine provision, the call to Christ would be a source of utter frustration, presenting the sorry spectacle of a sincere idealist, constantly thwarted by his own inadequacy.

If you will but trust Christ, not only for the death He died in order to redeem you, but also for the life that He lives and waits to live through you, the very next step you take will be a step taken in the very energy and power of God Himself. You will have begun to live a life which is essentially supernatural, yet still clothed with the common humanity of your physical body, and still worked out both in the big and the little things that inevitably make up the lot of a man who, though his heart may be with Christ in heaven, still has his two feet firmly planted on the earth.

You will have become *totally dependent* upon the life of Christ within you, and never before will you have been so *independent,* so *emancipated* from the pressure of your circumstances, so *released* at last from that self-distrust which has made you at one moment an arrogant, loud-mouthed braggart, and the next moment the victim of your own self-pity — and, either way, always in bondage to the fear of other men's opinions.

You will be free from the tyranny of a defeated enemy within. You will be more than conqueror, for even death itself is conquered by His life. Christ through death destroyed "him that had the power of death, that is, the devil" (Hebrews 2:14). This indeed is victory!

You will be restored to your true humanity — to be the human vehicle of the divine life. Your faith will open the windows of heaven, for God will move in to do the impossible, — and this is the speciality of creative Deity. Your friends will be baffled, for in reality you will have become a new creature — old things will have passed away, all things will have become new (II Corinthians 5:17). Through peace *with* God you will have found the peace *of* God, which "passeth all understanding."

Now if it is true that the Lord Jesus Christ will live His life through you on earth today, as He lived His life once in His own body on earth more than nineteen hundred years ago, it is both interesting and necessary to discover *how* He lived *then*, so that you may know *how* He will live through you *now*.

In John 6:56 it says, "He that eateth my flesh, and drinketh my blood, dwelleth in me, and I in him." From the context of this passage, we understand that the Lord Jesus Christ here uses the expression "to eat and to drink" as representing "to come and to believe," so that those that come *to* Him and believe *on* Him enter into a unique relationship *with* Him, — they dwell *in Him* and He dwells *in them*.

Verse 57 continues, "As the living Father hath sent me, and I live by the Father: so he that eateth me, even he shall live by me." As He lived by the Father, so you are to live by Him. How then did Jesus Christ live by the Father? Once you know the answer to this question, you will know thereafter how you are to live by Him, and at first the answer is surprising.

In John 5:19, Jesus said, "Verily, verily, I say unto you, The Son can do *nothing* of himself." Verse 28 of chapter 8 — "Then said Jesus unto them, When ye have lifted up the Son of man, then shall ye know that I am he, and that I do *nothing* of myself." Here we see Jesus Christ as man, living in total, unquestioning dependence upon the Father. Thus He fulfilled His true vocation as man, for He came in His sinless humanity to be what man through sin had ceased to be — the willing vehicle of the Divine Presence, allowing the Father to express Himself in action through His humanity.

Although Jesus Christ was Himself the Creative Deity, by whom all things were made, *as man* He humbled Himself — set aside His divine prerogatives and walked this earth *as man* — a perfect demonstration of what God intended man to be — the whole personality yielded to and occupied by God for Himself.

So the Lord Jesus prayed in John 17 verse 19, — "For their sakes I sanctify myself, that they also might be sanctified [*set wholly apart*] through the truth." That is to say, as He lived in unbroken dependence upon the Father, taking no step except in recognition of the fact that apart from the Father He could do nothing, so He calls upon you to live in the same total dependence upon Him — taking no step except in recognition of the fact that apart from Him, Christ, *you* can do nothing.

"I am the vine, ye are the branches: He that abideth in me, and I in him, the same bringeth forth much fruit: for *without me* ye can do *nothing*" (John 15:5). In other words, you can do no more without Him than He could do without the Father. But how much could the Father do through the Son? Everything! — for He was available to all that the Father made available to Him. "Jesus, knowing that the Father had given all things into his hands . . ." (John 13:3.) "It pleased the Father that in him should all fulness dwell" (Colossians 1:19).

How much then can Jesus Christ do through you and through me? Everything! He is limited only by the measure of our availability to all that He makes available to us, for "in him dwelleth all the fulness of the godhead bodily, and ye are complete in him" (Colossians 2:9, 10). What then is the faith that releases divine action? How may you be saved by His life, as you have already claimed to be redeemed by His death? This is the critical question of Christian experience, and the answer is simple — "The just shall live by faith" (Romans 1:17).

Faith in all its sheer simplicity! Faith that takes God precisely at His Word! Faith that simply says, "Thank You."

If you are to know the fulness of life in Christ, you are to appropriate the efficacy of *what He is* as you have already appropriated the efficacy of *what He has done*. Relate everything, moment by moment as it arises, to the adequacy of *what He is in you*, and assume that His adequacy will be operative; and on this basis in I Thessalonians 5:16 you are exhorted to "rejoice evermore!" You are to be incorrigibly cheerful, for you have solid grounds upon which to rejoice!

Again, "Pray without ceasing" (I Thessalonians 5:17), and here the word to pray does not mean to beg or to plead as if God were unwilling to give — but simply to expose by faith every situation as it arises, to the all-sufficiency of the One who indwells you by His life. Can any situation possibly arise, in any circumstances, for which He is not adequate? Any pressure, promise, problem, responsibility or temptation for which the Lord Jesus Himself is not adequate? If He be truly God, there cannot be a single one! "And (He is) declared to be the Son of God with power, according to the Spirit of holiness, by the resurrection from the dead" (Romans 1:4) — and of this, His resurrection life, we are made partakers!

This being so, applying His adequacy by faith to every situation as it arises, will leave you with no alternative but to obey the injunction of I Thessalonians 5:18—"In everything give thanks!" In how many things? In *everything* — without exception, "for this is the will of God in Christ Jesus concerning you."

If there is any situation from which you are not prepared to step back, in recognition of the total adequacy of Christ who is in you, then you are out of the will of God. You are asserting by your action and by your attitude that He has nothing to give you for that situation, which you do not have in yourself. This is the very negation of dependence, and you disobey the injunction of verse 19 — "Quench not the Spirit," for the office of the

Holy Spirit is to make known to you, and to make experiential to you, all that Christ is in you.

This, of course, is what it means to be filled with the Holy Spirit — to allow the Holy Spirit to occupy the whole of your personality with the adequacy of Christ. This is the sublime secret of drawing upon the unlimited resources of Deity. "Speaking to yourselves in psalms and hymns and spiritual songs, singing and making melody in your heart to the Lord; giving thanks always for all things unto God and the Father in the name of our Lord Jesus Christ" (Ephesians 5:19, 20).

How stupid it would be to buy a car with a powerful engine under the hood, and then to spend the rest of your days pushing it! Thwarted and exhausted, you would wish to discard it as a useless thing! Yet to some of you who are Christians, this may be God's word to your heart. When God redeemed you through the precious blood of His dear Son, He placed, in the language of my illustration, a powerful engine under the hood — nothing less than the resurrection life of God the Son, made over to you in the person of God the Holy Spirit. Then stop pushing! Step in and switch on, and expose every hill of circumstance, of opportunity, of temptation, of perplexity — no matter how threatening, — to the divine energy that is unfailingly available.

With what magnificent confidence you may step out into the future when once you have consented to die to your own self-effort, and to make yourself available as a redeemed sinner to all that God has made available to you in His risen Son!

To be *in Christ* — that is redemption; but for Christ to be *in you* — that is sanctification! To be *in Christ* — that makes you fit for heaven; but for Christ to be *in you* — that makes you fit for earth! To be *in Christ* — that changes your destination; but for Christ to be *in you* — that changes your destiny! The one makes heaven your home — the other makes this world His workshop.

I may wish to return to my home in England, and I stand in New York, but ever since I was born I have been bound to this earth by a law that I have never been able to break —

the law of gravity. I am told, however, that there is another law, a higher law, the law of aero-dynamics, and if only I will be willing to commit myself in total trust to this new law, then this new law will set me free from the old law. By faith I step into the plane, I sit back in the *rest* of faith, and as those mighty engines roar into life, I discover that the new law of aero-dynamics sets me free from the law of gravity.

So long as I maintain by faith that position of total dependence, I do not have to *try to be free* from the law of gravity — I am *being set free* by the operation of a new and a higher law. Of course, if I am stupid enough, way out across the Atlantic, I may decide that the cabin of the plane is too stuffy, and step out through the emergency window — but the moment I discard my position of faith in the new and higher law that is setting me free, I discover that the old down-drag is still fully in operation, and I am caught again by the law of gravity and plunged into the water!

I must maintain my attitude of dependence if I am to remain air-borne!

So you too are called upon by God to *walk* by faith, to *walk* in the Spirit, resting the whole weight of your personality upon the living Christ who is in you; and as by faith you walk in the Spirit, so God declares you will not fulfill the lusts of the flesh. You will be liberated, emancipated, set free from the down-drag of that inbred wickedness, which Christ alone can overcome. You will be made more than conqueror through "Christ, who is our life" (Colossians 3:4).

I wonder how it is with you? Have you ever put your trust in the Lord Jesus as your Redeemer? Have you been reconciled to God by the death of His Son? I wonder, if reconciled, whether you are at this moment being saved by His life? Have you learned to step out of every situation and relate it wholly to *what He is in you*, and by faith say "Thank You?"

Lord Jesus, how I thank Thee that Thou hast not only redeemed me with Thy precious blood, reconciled me to God and established peace between my guilty soul and God my Maker, but I thank Thee that Thou art risen from the dead,

that at this very moment Thou dost indwell me in the person
and power of Thy divine Spirit; that Thou hast never expected
of me anything but failure, yet Thou has given to me Thy
strength for my weakness, Thy victory for my defeat, Thyself
for all my bankruptcy! I step out now by faith, into a future
that is limited only by what Thou art! To me to live is Christ!
For Thy Name's sake. Amen.

A New Principle

2

A New Principle

WE HAVE BEGUN TO SEE THAT VICTORIOUS CHRISTIAN LIVING IS not a method or technique; it is an entirely different, revolutionary principle of life. It is the principle of an *exchanged* life — ". . . not I, but Christ liveth in me" (Galatians 2:20).

This is all part of our Gospel — it is not the Gospel *plus!* We must not get our terminology wrong. To divorce the behavior of the Christian from the Gospel is entirely false and is not true to the Word of God, yet all too often such is the characteristic of gospel preaching.

I would like to explore with you what is the true spiritual content of our Gospel — not just heaven *one day,* but Christ *right now!* Christ *in you,* on the grounds of redemption — this is the Gospel! To preach anything less than this must inevitably produce "Evan-jellyfish" — folk with no spiritual vertebrae, whose faith does not "behave!"

Do you remember what James says in his epistle? "As the body without the spirit is dead, so faith without works is dead" (chapter 2:26). The "spirit" there means breath, and a body without breath is dead. Stop breathing — and folk will bury you! In other words, a *living body* breathes, and a *living faith* breathes, and a living faith breathes with *divine action.* A living faith breathes with the activity of Jesus Christ. That is why the Lord Jesus, in John 6:29, said, "This is the work of God, that ye believe on him whom he hath sent."

That is the work of God. It is your living faith in the adequacy of the One who is *in you,* which releases His divine action *through you.* It is the kind of activity that the Bible calls "good works," as opposed to "dead works."

25

"Good works" are those works that have their origin in Jesus Christ — whose activity is released through your body, presented to Him as a living sacrifice by a faith that expresses total dependence, as opposed to the Adamic independence (Romans 12:1, 2).

There are two very simple illustrations given to us in the Old Testament of these two facets of the truth — "you in Christ" and "Christ in you." We will glance at them briefly because there is no better Bible commentary in all the world than the Bible itself! If you want to know what the Bible means, then turn to the Bible and it will tell you — and you are not likely to be confused!

> Exodus 15:22-26 — "So Moses brought Israel from the Red Sea, and they went out into the wilderness of Shur; and they went three days in the wilderness, and found no water And when they came to Marah, they could not drink of the waters of Marah, for they were bitter; therefore the name of it was called Marah [a word that means *bitterness*]. And the people murmured against Moses, saying, What shall we drink? And he cried unto the Lord; and the Lord showed him a tree, which when he had cast into the waters, the waters were made sweet; there he made for them a statute and an ordinance, and there he proved them, and said, If thou wilt diligently hearken to the voice of the Lord thy God, and wilt do that which is right in his sight, and wilt give ear to his commandments, and keep all his statutes, I will put none of these diseases upon thee, which I have brought upon the Egyptians: for I am the Lord that healeth thee."

The incident concerns God's divine intervention in bringing His people out of Egypt. We will not pause to consider that now as we shall be doing so later, suffice it to recognize that this particular incident is just an underlining, an emphasis of the redemptive principle. This is the first picture — bitter waters in which there was only death, and they cried to God and God showed them a tree.

The meaning, of course, is obvious, for there had come a day when Adam fell into sin, and how dark and how deep and how bitter had the waters become within the soul of man! All the tears, and all the anguish, and all the sorrow, and all the death, and all the crying, and all the dying — this has been the consequence of that first Adamic repudiation of man's true relationship to God, of which you and I today are still the heirs, in this poor, sin-sick world!

The waters indeed are dark and deep and bitter within the soul of man, but the Spirit of God moves upon the face of the waters, and they are stirred, and the soul is awakened, and at last the soul, convicted of its sin, cries out to God, and He says, "Behold the lamb of God, which taketh away the sin of the world" (John 1:29).

He showed them a tree! ". . . which when he had cast into the waters, the waters were made sweet." He bore our sins "in His own body on the tree" (I Peter 2:24). This was the *second* tree, the place of *second choice,* for as Adam had repudiated his relationship to God at that first tree, and said "No" to God, and stepped out of life into death, out of dependence into independence — so may you and I at that second tree, the place of second choice, say our "Yes" where he said "No." Step back out of death into life! Be raised from the dead — out of our self-will and independence, into a childlike *dependence* — the obedience of faith.

"I am the Lord that healeth thee." This is the beginning of our salvation! This is to be reconciled to God by the death of His Son.

It is " the tree for bitterness" — the precious blood of the Lord Jesus that cleanses us from all sin, and though our sins be as scarlet, they shall be as white as snow; though they are red like crimson, they shall be as wool. This is the beginning of our faith, and this is where we must begin — for if we have not begun here, we have not begun at all. But it would be a very sad thing to stop there!

That is why we have this other very valuable picture. It is found this time in II Kings 2:19: "And the men of the city said unto Elisha, Behold, I pray thee, the situation of this city is pleasant as my lord seeth: but the water is naught, and the ground barren." This is a different picture.

Here is a beautiful city, enchantingly situated. The casual passer-by, the stranger, the traveler, the merchant — they would be glad to sojourn awhile, to spend the night, or, if possible, the weekend. They would like to come back for their vacation with the family! They would congratulate the inhabitants on the good fortune that was theirs to live in such attractive surroundings; and yet, beneath all this charming exterior, there was heartbreak, a sickening load within the breasts of those who lived there.

They showed a brave face when folk congratulated them; and when folk admired their beautiful city, they displayed a sweet smile; they tried not to give their inner sorrow away, yet every time somebody admired and flattered the place where they lived, it hurt them! They knew the inner secret: "The water was naught, and the ground was barren."

When it says "the water was naught," it does not mean that there was no water, as we shall discover; but it was stale and stagnant, producing sterility! When it says "the ground was barren," it does not mean to say that nothing grew — otherwise the place would not have looked so charming. The word "barren" means "causing to miscarry."

Had you been there in the early Spring, you would have seen all the early evidences of coming harvest. You would have seen the tiny, tender shoots bursting through the soil. You would have seen the leaves beginning to pop out of the buds on the trees and bushes, and a week or two later you would have seen the blossom fashion, fade, and fall, to leave the promise of a bumper crop. You might well have congratulated the people on all that they had, seemingly, to look forward to.

That was the tragedy of it! Maybe there still lurked in the hearts of the inhabitants the feeble hope that this year things would be different — that maybe they had turned the corner and that everything was now to be all right — yet something, heavy as lead, deep down in their hearts, kept saying "No! it will always be just the same! You know exactly what is going to happen!" And it did! It always happened! The fruit, just about to ripen, ready to be plucked, fell suddenly to the ground — premature and immature — to rot and never to reproduce. This was the heartbreak of that beautiful city! So deceptive! So impressive to everybody except to those who lived there! Of what is this a picture?

It may, of course, be a picture of *you!* Do not be shocked when I say it — it is the picture of a carnal Christian. You say, "I thought a carnal Christian was a backslider — somebody, for

instance, who used to go to church, but has run off with somebody else's wife!" Oh no! That is only one kind of carnal
Christian, and I would not suggest that you were that kind of
carnal Christian.

No, no! I am talking about Sunday school teachers. I
am talking about some Sunday school superintendents. I am talking about some pastor in his pulpit. I am talking about some
missionary on the field. I am talking about many ordinary, average, earnest Christians. They are wonderful people. You
would love to meet them. They talk all the language of salvation and they mean every word they say. They are not hypocrites! They are tired, many of them — desperately tired! God
knows how tired they are, but they are not hypocrites.

They are overwhelmed inwardly with a sense of defeat,
and frustration, and futility, and barrenness — but when you
meet them, they will smile sweetly and they will mean the smile
they give you. They will grip you by the hand and they will
say, "God bless you for passing my way!" They will thank you
for all the encouragement that you have given them; yet, as you
thank them for the message you have just heard from their lips,
your very words of thanks will hurt them, because they know
what you do *not* know — that for years they have labored in
vain!

The fruit that has appeared to others has fallen — oh, so
often, so *cruelly* often — to the ground — premature, immature
— only to rot and never to reproduce.

Story after story could be told of men and women who
bravely, doggedly, out of a sense of duty, love, and devotion, go
on, and on, and on — yet deep down in their hearts they are
tired, almost beyond endurance! Again and again they have got
down by their bedside and cried out to God, with tears in their
eyes; "God, You know how barren I am, You know how empty
I am, You know how stale I am, You *know* it!" — and yet they
do not know the answer.

I wonder, are you like that?

At last the burden became intolerable and the men of
the city came to the man of God and they poured out the whole
story. "He said, Bring me a new cruse, and put salt therein. And

they brought it to him. And he went forth unto the spring of the waters, and cast the salt in there, and said, Thus saith the Lord, I have healed these waters; there shall not be from thence any more death or barren land. So the waters were healed unto this day, according to the saying of Elisha which he spake" (II Kings 2:20-22). He went to the spring of the waters — for there *were* waters — and he placed salt at the source. What does salt represent?

Salt speaks of the risen life of the glorified Saviour, imparted by the indwelling of the Holy Spirit to the redeemed sinner. It is the *tree* for bitterness! It is the *salt* for barrenness! As you have been reconciled to God by His *death*, so you are constantly to be saved by His *life*.

It is only the life of the Lord Jesus — His activity, *clothed* with you and *displayed* through you, that ultimately will find the approval of God. As a forgiven sinner, you are a member of "an holy priesthood, to offer up spiritual sacrifices, acceptable to God by Jesus Christ" (I Peter 2:5). It is the Lord Jesus Christ alone who makes your sacrifices acceptable to God. Only what He does in you and through you merits His approval, and God can, and will, accept nothing less!

"And every oblation of thy meat-offering shalt thou season with salt; neither shalt thou suffer the salt of the covenant of thy God to be lacking from thy meat-offering: with all thine offerings thou shalt offer salt" (Leviticus 2:13). *Under no circumstances*, God said in His law given to Moses, were any offerings to be brought to Him, or sacrifices made, that were not seasoned with salt. Without the salt they would not be acceptable, no matter how sincerely brought, no matter at how great a cost, no matter how lofty the motive, no matter how noble the ideal; without salt they would not be acceptable.

This was the practice, as in Ezekiel 43:24. "Thou shalt offer (these offerings) before the Lord, and the priests shall cast salt upon them, and they shall offer them up for a burnt-offering unto the Lord." It was salt that made the offering acceptable.

Now the Lord Jesus, in Luke 14:33, tells us the minimum demands that He makes for true discipleship. He says, "Whosoever he be of you that forsaketh not all that he hath [literally *all that he hath* — himself, and all that he possesses], he cannot be my disciple." He has got to recognize his bankruptcy, so that his sole wealth is vested in the One whom God has credited to him in the person and by the presence of His divine Spirit. This is the condition for discipleship.

"Salt," He goes on to say in verse 34, "is good; but if the salt have lost his savour, wherewith shall it be seasoned? It is neither fit for the land, nor yet for the dunghill; but men cast it out. He that hath ears to hear, let him hear." There is a substitute salt that has lost its savour. In the Middle East, salt is at a premium. I served there in the Army during the war and we did good business! For some reason, salt is scarce and the Arabs would give anything for a pinch of salt. You could get a dozen eggs, you could buy a chicken, you could have bought their shirt, for a pinch of salt! I do not think you would have wanted the shirt, as you would not have known which hole to put your arms through! But salt was everything to them, because with salt they preserved their meat and their fish.

Because salt was scarce, however, there were substitutes on the market — good to the taste, all right for immediate consumption, but the moment they tried to preserve their food with these substitutes, to keep it pure and healthy, and edible, within a matter of hours, or at most a matter of days in that hot, sultry climate, it went putrid and bad and stank! It was not even fit for the dunghill!

As in the case of substitute salt, there is a *form of activity* that is all right for immediate consumption. It impresses everybody, your stock goes high — but it will always leave a stink behind it, if it stems from the flesh! If it is self-activity! It will always produce the kind of fruit that drops, both premature and immature — to rot, and never to reproduce!

This is the work of God, that you believe, and maintain unrelentingly, total dependence upon the One whom God has sent to fill you with Himself. He is the true Salt, through whom you are made the salt of the earth.

Here is another, fascinating reference to salt. It is described in Leviticus 2:13 as the "salt of the covenant," the token of God's unfailing pledge and purpose in the lives of redeemed sinners — ". . . accepted in the beloved. In whom we have redemption through his blood, the forgiveness of sins, according to the riches of his grace" (Ephesians 1:6, 7). That is the tree for bitterness! "In whom ye also trusted . . . in whom also after that ye believed, ye were sealed with that Holy Spirit of promise, which is the earnest [or *guarantee*] of our inheritance . . ." (Ephesians 1:13). That is the salt of the covenant — the salt for barrenness! The resurrection life of the Lord Jesus imparted to the true believer by the presence of the Holy Spirit!

The Lord Jesus said, "He that believeth on me, as the Scripture hath said, out of his innermost being shall flow rivers of living [*not stagnant!*] water." (But this spake he of the Spirit, which they that believe on him should receive: for the Holy Ghost was not yet given; because that Jesus was not yet glorified) (John 7:38, 39). That is to say, salt at the source! Salt at "the spring of the waters" (II Kings 2:21).

Ezra 7:6: "This Ezra went up from Babylon; and he was a ready scribe in the law of Moses, which the Lord God of Israel had given: and the king granted him all his request, according to the hand of the Lord his God upon him." It is a wonderful thing to be in such a relationship to God that everything you need, for any circumstance, is always yours, by the good hand of your God upon you! "For Ezra had prepared his heart to seek the law of the Lord, and to do it, and to teach in Israel statutes and judgments." He had said in his heart, "I am going to seek the mind of God in the Word of God, do the will of God, and teach the ways of God" (verse 10), and for this reason he was among those whom God raised up to rebuild, cleanse, and fill the temple with the worship of God.

The king gave him a letter. He said, "I, even I Artaxerxes the king, do make a decree to all the treasurers which are beyond the river, that whatsoever Ezra the priest, the scribe of the law of the God of heaven, shall require of you, it be done speedily" (verse 21). What had Ezra asked for, that pure worship might be re-established in the cleansed House of God? "Unto an hundred talents of silver, and to an hundred measures of wheat, and to an hundred baths of wine, and to an hundred baths of oil, *and salt without prescribing how much!*" He said, in so many words, "King Artaxerxes, I want a hundred of this, I want a hundred of that, and I want a hundred of the other; but I must have *unlimited quantities of salt!* I must never run out of salt — because no matter how costly, no matter how sacrificial, no matter how sincere, God will accept *nothing* that is not seasoned with salt! I must have *unlimited quantities of salt!*"

Now is that not a wonderful picture? And God has given you unlimited quantities of salt! "For God is able to make *all* grace abound toward you; that ye, *always* having *all* sufficiency in *all* things, may abound to *every* good work" (II Corinthians 9:8).

Is it this Salt that you need? Then prepare your heart, with Ezra of old, "to seek the law of the Lord and to do it," and know that Jesus Christ Himself is all you need, in death and resurrection, to cleanse and fill you, and hear Him say, "Thus saith the Lord, I have healed these waters; there shall not be from thence any more death or barren land" (II Kings 2:21).

Three Categories of Men

3

Three Categories of Men

ONE OF THE MOST REMARKABLE EPISODES IN THE BIBLE IS THE story of how God brought His people Israel out of Egypt, through the wilderness, and into the land of Canaan. It is as though the Holy Spirit gave us here a master key, a point of reference, a framework into which are woven all the mighty colored threads of truth. It will be my purpose to examine with you what it means to be in the land of Egypt, what it means to be in the wilderness, and what it means to be in Canaan. Over four hundred years the children of Israel had been enslaved by the Egyptians, suffering bitterly beneath burdens inflicted by their taskmasters, helpless to save themselves, hopeless but for the fact that four hundred years before, God had promised Abraham that He would act to redeem them. This is the picture God gives us of the unforgiven sinner.

At the fall of man, when Adam sinned, God withdrew His Holy Spirit from the human spirit, and although man retained his animal body and possessed still a functioning soul of mind, emotion and will, he was empty of God. Spiritually bankrupt, man was destitute of that spiritual life which could be his only by virtue of God's presence, through His Holy Spirit, within the human spirit. God had left him!

This was the consequence of sin — the absence of all spiritual life. As the absence of all physical life means physical death, so the absence of all spiritual life means spiritual death. This is the wages of sin; not the ultimate consequence of sin *one day,* but that which has been the consequence of sin ever since man fell, and is now the consequence of sin to all who have not as yet been saved from this condition, for it is in this condition of spiritual death that we are all born, easy prey to the ravages of a sin principle that came into the human heart in the day that God went out.

This sin principle is called in the Bible, "the flesh." This is not the human body, which in itself is not sinful, but the flesh in this biblical sense speaks of an evil bias, a satanic agency from which springs all man's own inbred wickedness, so that in Mark 7:20-23, the Lord Jesus said, "That which cometh out of the man, that defileth the man. For from within, out of the heart of men, proceed evil thoughts, adulteries, fornications, murders, thefts, covetousness, wickedness, deceit, lasciviousness, an evil eye, blasphemy, pride, foolishness: All these evil things come from within, and defile the man."

Here the Lord Jesus Christ is speaking about "the flesh," this satanic agency, this sin principle, and just as the land of Egypt represents our natural condition of spiritual death, so the Egyptian taskmasters represent the flesh in its tyrannical control over human behavior, so that Paul, in Romans 7:19 and 20, writes, "For the good that I would I do not: but the evil which I would not, that I do. Now if I do that I would not, it is no more I that do it, but *sin* that dwelleth in me." "Sin," in this sense, as a singular word, is the same thing as "the flesh" — the root that bears the fruit. And in this our flesh dwells no good thing! It is "enmity against God: for it is not subject to the law of God, neither indeed can be" (Romans 8:7).

It is quite obvious that it is no more God's purpose for you to remain in this condition of spiritual destitution and defeat than it was God's purpose for His earthly people, Israel, to remain in the land of Egypt, tyrannized by Egyptian taskmasters. It is not surprising, therefore, that in this story there is great stress laid upon the means which God employed to get His people *out* of Egypt.

God raised up Moses, and through him He commanded the people to take a little lamb without blemish, and to slay it — but without breaking a bone thereof. The blood of this little lamb was then to be painted on the doorposts and on the lintel of every home, and this was to be known later as the Passover, for in the night that the lamb was slain, God executed judg-

ment upon the Egyptians, so that all the first-born in the land of
Egypt died, from the first-born of Pharaoh that sat upon his
throne, to the first-born of beasts. God's plan for Israel was this:

The blood shall be to you for a token upon the houses where you are:
and when I see the blood, I will pass over you, and the plague shall not
be upon you to destroy you, when I smite the land of Egypt. And this
day shall be unto you for a memorial; and ye shall keep it a feast to the
Lord throughout your generations; ye shall keep it a feast by an ordin-
ance for ever (Exodus 12:13, 14).

This picture foreshadowed the death of Christ upon the
cross, for He was declared by John the Baptist to be "the Lamb
of God which taketh away the sin of the world" (John 1:29),
or as in I Corinthians 5:7 — "Christ our passover is sacrificed
for us."

Just as the little lamb bore the judgment in the place of
the first-born in the house of Israel, so Jesus Christ bore our sins
in His own body on the tree at Calvary. I Peter 3:18 tells us
that He suffered "the just for the unjust, that He might bring
us to God." This is God's plan of redemption. When the Lord
Jesus Christ died upon the cross, God executed judgment upon
your sin in *His* person. Of His own free will He took your place
in death, that you might be reconciled to God, a forgiven sinner.

All that God asked His people Israel to do was to apply
the blood to the doorposts and to the lintels *by faith,* and then
rest in God's promise. All that God asks *you* to do is to apply the
death of Christ to your own need as a guilty sinner, by faith,
then rest in God's promise of forgiveness and humbly say,
"Thank You."

The story goes on to tell us that as God's judgment de-
scended upon Egypt that night, God, by the hand of Moses, led
His people out from Egypt and through the Red Sea. Because
of God's miraculous intervention, the Israelites went through the
Red Sea on dry land, but when the Egyptians tried to follow,
they were drowned. So the enemy was buried in the place of
death, while God's people passed on *through* the place of death
into a new land and on to a new life.

There is a significant passage in I Corinthians 10. In the
first two verses we read, "Moreover, brethren, I would not that
ye should be ignorant, how that all our fathers were under the

cloud, and all passed through the sea, and were all baptized unto Moses in the cloud and in the sea." Here Paul describes the children of Israel as having been baptized into Moses, for on that day they followed him into the Red Sea, which would have been a place of death had not God divided the waters and brought them miraculously out of this place of death, on to dry land. This must be compared with Romans 6, for there we read in the third verse, "Know ye not, that so many of us as were baptized into Jesus Christ, were baptized into His death? Therefore we are buried with Him by baptism into death; that like as Christ was raised up from the dead . . . even so we also should walk in newness of life."

In other words, just as the Egyptian taskmasters were left buried in the place of death, from which the children of Israel had been raised miraculously by God, so as you and I identify ourselves by faith with Jesus Christ, in God's economy we go with Him, spiritually, into the place of death, leaving this old sin nature called the flesh buried with Him there.

We may understand again, therefore, from this picture, that God's purpose in the cross of Jesus Christ was two-fold: first that we might be forgiven, being saved from sin's penalty because Christ died *for us,* and secondly, that we might be delivered from sin's power, because this old sinful nature, called the flesh, died *with Him.*

The question that must arise quite naturally now is this, "If in God's economy my old nature has been crucified with Christ, and I am to reckon upon this by faith as a fact, what is to take its place as the controlling principle of my life?" The Bible answer is to be found in Galatians 4:4 — "When the fulness of the time was come, God sent forth his Son, made of a woman, made under the law, to redeem them that were under the law, that we might receive the adoption of sons. And because ye are sons, God hath sent forth the *Spirit of his Son into your hearts,* crying, Abba, Father." That is to say, no sooner are you redeemed, because you have put your faith in the One who died for you, than God restores to your human spirit the presence of the Holy Spirit, by whose presence you receive the very life of the Lord Jesus, risen from the dead, and become in Him a partaker of the divine nature.

In II Peter 1:3, 4, we read, "According as his divine power hath given unto us all things that pertain unto life and godliness, through the knowledge of him that hath called us to glory and virtue: Whereby are given unto us exceeding great and precious promises, that by these ye might be partakers of the divine nature."

I may say to a glove, "Glove, pick up this Bible," and yet, somehow, the glove cannot do it. It has got a thumb and fingers, the shape and form of a hand, and yet it is unable to do the thing I command it to do. You may say, "Well, of course not. You have never told the glove how!" But I may preach to and instruct that glove until my patience is exhausted, but the glove, try as it will, still cannot pick up that Bible. Yet I have a glove at home that has picked up my Bible dozens of times! — but never once before I put my hand into it! As soon, however, as my hand comes into that glove, the glove becomes as strong as my hand. Everything possible to my hand becomes possible to that glove — but only in the measure in which the glove is prepared simply to clothe the activity of my hand.

That is what it is to have Christ, by His Spirit, dwelling within your redeemed humanity. You are the glove, Christ is the Hand! Everything that is possible to Him becomes possible to you, and with Paul you may say, "I have strength for all things in Christ Who empowers me — I am ready for anything and equal to anything through Him Who infuses inner strength into me, [that is, I am self-sufficient in Christ's sufficiency]" (Philippians 4:13 *Amplified New Testament*). The presence of the living Christ, by His Spirit within you, imparts to you all the things that pertain to life and godliness, all that you need to live a life of righteousness and nobility of character.

It is this enjoyment of Christ's indwelling which is represented by the land of Canaan; the land of promise and of plentiful provision.

Canaan in the Bible is not heaven. It is not "pie in the sky when I die." It is *Christ Himself,* and *right now,* living His victorious life through me. Indeed, it is only the Lord

Jesus Christ Himself who is capable of living the Christian life; as Romans 5:10 declares, He not only reconciles you to God by His death, but He saves you moment by moment by His life; that is to say, He died not only for what you *have done,* but He rose again to live in you, to take the place of *what you are.* His strength for your weakness! His wisdom for your folly! His drive for your drift! His grace for your greed! His love for your lust! His peace for your problems! His joy for your sorrow! His plenty for your poverty! *This* is Canaan!

> Out of my bondage, sorrow, and night . . . .
> Into Thy freedom, gladness, and light . . . .
> Out of my sickness into Thy health,
> Out of my want and into Thy wealth,
> Out of my sin and into Thyself,
> Jesus, I come to Thee!

This is Canaan! Brought *out* to be brought *in!*

This was God's purpose for His people *then,* and this is God's purpose for His redeemed people *now.* He desires that the *natural man* — destitute of divine life, the devil's plaything, destined for hell — might become the *spiritual man* — filled with the Spirit of Christ, alive unto God as an instrument of righteousness, destined for heaven!

Why then the wilderness?

This is the tragedy of Christendom today, as it was the tragedy of God's people Israel then, for forty years in the wilderness. A people who lived in self-imposed poverty! Every day they spent in the desert was a day they could have spent in Canaan — for God had given them the land! They would not believe, however, that the God who brought them out was the God who could bring them in!

The wilderness is a picture of what the New Testament describes as a carnal Christian. If you are a carnal Christian, it means that you have been redeemed by faith in Christ through His reconciling death; you have received the gift of the Holy Spirit by whose gracious presence Christ lives within you, but you live, in spite of this, in self-imposed poverty, under the subtle influences of a defeated foe, the flesh, which Christ took with Him into the grave. You are just like the children of Israel who lived for forty years, plagued by the memories and the subtle influences of an enemy whom God buried to the last man in the depths of the Red Sea. You, as they, enjoy neither the flesh pots of Egypt, nor the golden corn of Canaan — you are dumped in the desert!

The unbelief of the children of Israel cheated them of that for which they had been brought out of Egypt. They lived only to discredit the good name of the One who had redeemed them. In the same way, there is nothing quite so pathetic as a Christian who has been vested with "all the fulness of the Godhead bodily" in Christ, and to whom has been made available all the illimitable resources of heaven, yet who in ignorance, or in defiance of this fact, stretches out a mere existence in the meager resources which he brings with him out of the Egypt of his unbelief, with no sense of direction or finality of purpose — for he will not take what God has *given!*

Forty weary years it took before God was able, through Joshua, to teach His people that to *get in* takes precisely the same kind of faith that it takes to *get out* — the faith that trusts God and says "Thank You"! When once they stood by faith with their feet in the waters of Jordan, the God who divided the Red Sea divided the Jordan also and brought them through on dry land to possess at last their possessions.

The carnal Christian is the one who has received the Holy Spirit and all the fulness of Christ, yet ignores His presence and struggles to live the Christian life as though Christ were not there. He is the one who constantly begs and pleads for all that God has already given him, but which he will not take. He is the one who will not step out by faith upon the glorious fact that Christ is his life, and therefore his victory!

The Christian life is an exchanged life. "I am crucified with Christ, nevertheless I live, *yet not I,* but Christ liveth in me" (Galatians 2:20). "To me to live is Christ" (Philippians 1:21). Three categories of men! In Egypt, in the wilderness, or in Canaan. I wonder — in which category are you?

Are you still in Egypt? Then trust Christ *now* as your Saviour! By faith, *now,* apply the precious blood that He shed upon the cross, to the doorposts and lintel of your own heart, and thank Him like a child that you are redeemed!

Are you still in the wilderness? Then repudiate your unbelief! Start right now trusting the Lord Jesus for that for which His blood was shed — that He might live His resurrection life in and through you, even while you are still on earth in the body, and thank Him that He *is* your victory, that He *is* your strength, that He *is* your future, that He is *all* that you can *ever* need at *any* time, in *any* circumstances, for "in him dwelleth all the fulness of the Godhead bodily, and you are complete in him" (Colossians 2:9, 10).

Are you in the Promised Land? Then your portion is to reign in life! To reign by One, Christ Jesus, and to know joy unspeakable and full of glory, to know His peace that passeth all understanding, to know that every place that the sole of your foot shall tread upon has been given to you, that you may be strong and of a good courage, neither afraid nor dismayed, in the knowledge that the Lord your God is with you whithersoever you go, for this — *this* is your victory, "even your faith" (I John 5:4).

Dear Lord Jesus Christ, I thank Thee for dying upon the cross for me, a guilty sinner. I accept Thee gladly as my Saviour, to redeem me now, — to cleanse and to forgive me now. Come by Thy gracious Holy Spirit to live in me, that I may be born again, a child of God — now! This is Thy promise, and that is enough for me. I know I am redeemed! Thou art my very life, all that I can ever need at any time! Thou wilt never leave me nor forsake me, but ever guide me and keep me — Christ my Saviour, my Lord, my God, my life — forever! Amen.

A Day to Be Remembered

4

A Day to Be Remembered

HAVING VIEWED IN GENERAL IN THE PRECEDING CHAPTER, THIS
"spiritual master key" as seen in the early history of Israel, I
would like in these succeeding chapters to examine the story in
closer detail. This must involve, inevitably, a certain amount of
recapitulation.

In the twelfth chapter of Exodus the Lord spoke to
Moses and said, "This month shall be unto you the beginning of
months: it shall be the first month of the year to you. Speak ye
unto all the congregation of Israel, saying, In the tenth day of
this month they shall take to them every man a lamb, according
to the house of their fathers, a lamb for an house. . . ."

This month would see the dawn of a day of such significance that it would herald an entirely new era in the lives of the
children of Israel. It would be as though they had never lived
before! It would be a day indeed to be remembered!

I need hardly explain to you that the day to be con-
sidered here is a picture of that day when a man enters into
peace with God, becomes reconciled on God's terms, and finds
salvation. He is redeemed!

Can you look back to the day when you were redeemed?
Have you a day to be remembered?

I can look back to that day when, as a boy of twelve, I
accepted Jesus Christ as my Saviour. I remember the hour! I
could almost take you to the very spot! A quarter to nine, on a
Saturday night, in a boys' camp in August. And nobody knew,
apart from myself and the Christ who redeemed me! But I know
that *that* day was the beginning of days for me; and *that* month
was the first month of a new life! I can hardly remember any-

thing that happened before my twelfth year — it was just as though I had only existed, and then suddenly I had begun to live, for it was the beginning of life as God intended life to be. It was a day to be remembered!

"Your lamb shall be without blemish, a male of the first year . . . and the whole assembly of the congregation of Israel shall kill it in the evening. And they shall take of the blood, and strike it on the two side posts and on the upper door post of the houses wherein they shall eat it" (Exodus 12:5-7).

This is one of the most beautiful pictures of our redemption that we have in the Word of God. The Holy Spirit leaves us in no doubt as to the spiritual significance of the Passover lamb, for in I Corinthians 5:7 we read, ". . . Christ our passover is sacrificed for us." He is "the Lamb of God that taketh away the sin of the world," and only those who are sheltered beneath His shed blood can ever escape the final judgment that God in His holiness must execute upon sin and the sinful seed of Adam.

The picture is clear. Recognizing your guilty condition before a holy God, and humbly recognizing Jesus Christ, the One in whom your sin was executed once for all, you mix with faith this word of reconciliation, and cast yourself upon Him, and you are redeemed! By faith you apply the precious blood of the Lamb to the doorposts and the lintel of your heart, and the wrath of God passes over you. This represents the vicarious sacrifice of Jesus Christ, His substitutionary work whereby He was made sin for you, that you might be made the righteousness of God in Him (II Corinthians 5:21). This is the beginning of days! This is where life begins! Can you look back to that moment when, as a guilty sinner, you humbly confessed your need and claimed Jesus Christ as your Saviour, the One in whom alone you may find peace with a holy God?

Notice how the passover was celebrated. Exodus 12:11 — "Thus shall ye eat it; with your loins girded, your shoes on your feet, and your staff in your hand; and ye shall eat it in haste." In the day that the blood was applied, they had to be equipped for a journey, for that day was to be to them the threshold of a journey. It was not just to be a critical experience, one to be enjoyed and then forgotten, or something ecstatic which would become a fond memory of the past! The passover was to be the *beginning* — the *means*, not the *end!* From this day they could never be the same again — they were to embark upon a journey!

Now this, of course, is vitally important, and in Romans chapter 8, from verse 1 onward, there is the spiritual counterpart in the New Testament — "There is therefore now no condemnation to them which are in Christ Jesus, who *walk* not after the flesh but after the Spirit." In other words, the New Testament definition of a man who is "IN CHRIST JESUS," and who can claim that there is therefore now no condemnation for him, is a man who has been precipitated by the crisis of redemption into a NEW WALK — "not after the flesh but after the Spirit."

The claim that you are in Christ Jesus, and under no condemnation because you have been redeemed, is only valid if it is vindicated by a walk that indicates your new relationship to God.

I know of no gospel in the Bible that offers you salvation from the condemnation of your sin, that does not at the same time demand a radical change of walk! A walk under entirely new management, revolutionized according to an entirely new principle of life; and this we see beautifully illustrated in the story that we are now considering.

In a Land to Be Possessed

They were to eat the Passover on this first occasion girded for a journey — a journey which would take them *out* of Egypt and *into* Canaan. Exodus 13:3 — "And Moses said unto the people, Remember this day, in which ye came out from Egypt, out of the house of bondage; for by strength of hand the Lord brought you out from this place. . . . And it shall be" (verse 5) "when the Lord shall bring thee into the land of the Canaanites . . . which He sware unto thy fathers to give thee, a land flowing with milk and honey, that thou shalt keep this service in this month." It was a day to be remembered — but *in a land to be possessed!*

Only in the *land* could the people celebrate the day intelligently! They came out from Egypt which, as we have already seen, is the Bible picture of the unregenerate condition of the unforgiven sinner — the first category of men; but God brought them out that He might bring them into the land of Canaan, the

Bible picture of the Spirit-filled, victorious Christian — the third category of men.

Do not be deceived by the false significance given to Canaan in so much popular hymnology composed, no doubt quite sincerely, but by those who have mistaken the issues and missed the point. Remember — as has already been explained — Canaan is Christ *now*, *NOT* heaven *one day!*

There is only one place where you can intelligently celebrate your redemption through the death of Jesus Christ, and that is in the fulness of His resurrection life! This is a spiritual principle!

It was a day to be remembered in a land to be possessed!

"And thou shalt show thy son in that day saying, This is done because of that which the Lord did unto me when I came forth out of Egypt." Can you imagine how unimpressed a small boy would be in the middle of the desert if his father told him, in answer to his question, that the Passover feast was in celebration of their deliverance out of Egypt?

Manna for breakfast — manna for lunch — manna for supper! This poor kid had had that for thirteen years or more and everybody knew what he would get for breakfast the next morning! I think he would be inclined to say, "Dad, if this is all we are celebrating, isn't it time we got back into Egypt? I've heard what it was like in Egypt, and it sounds much more attractive to me than here in the desert!"

I wonder if this is why so many children grow up unconverted in Christian homes? I wonder if it is because so many Christian parents are living in the wilderness? They have demonstrated so little to their children of what it means to walk in the plenitude of the risen Christ that "the kids" inevitably glance back over their shoulders in search of relief from the monotony of a desert diet!

The Passover, together with two other feasts, was to be celebrated *yearly* from the day that God brought them out. Exodus 23:14 — "Three times thou shalt keep a feast unto me in the year. Thou shalt keep the feast of unleavened bread: (thou shalt eat unleavened bread seven days, as I commanded thee, in the time appointed of the month Abib; for in it thou camest out of Egypt

. . .)" — you are to remember the day that God redeemed you!
Verse 16: "And the feast of harvest, the firstfruits of thy labours,
which thou hast sown in the field: and the feast of ingathering,
which is in the end of the year, when thou has gathered in thy
labours out of the field." These three feasts were to be celebrated
yearly by God's redeemed people — the feast of unleavened bread
(the Passover), the feast of harvest, and the feast of ingathering.
The harvest of that "which they had sown in the field" — how
much did they sow in the desert? Nothing! How much did they
ingather in the desert? Nothing! How much corn had they in the
desert with which to keep the feast of unleavened bread? None!
How then could the people of Israel keep yearly these three feasts
in the wilderness? They could not! Because it was a day to be
remembered *in a land to be possessed!*

I can discover only one account of the Passover feast
having been celebrated in the wilderness and that was in the
second year. Numbers 9:1 — "The Lord spake unto Moses in the
wilderness of Sinai, in the first month of the second year after
they were come out of the land of Egypt, saying, Let the children
of Israel also keep the passover at his appointed season." That is
the only record I find of their ever having celebrated the Passover
in the wilderness, and with what did they celebrate it? Only with
the corn which they must have brought with them out of Egypt!
That is significant, because unless you go on into the fulness of
what Christ is in you, you will only be able to celebrate your con-
version with such meager, poverty-stricken resources as you
brought with you out of your unregenerate condition; in other
words, the "energy of the flesh," and this, you will discover, will
last just about twelve months and then you will be exhausted!

Exodus 13:9 — "It shall be for a sign unto thee upon
thine hand" — the Passover is to represent that your redemption
"out of Egypt" has changed the things you do. "It shall be for a
memorial between thine eyes"—it is to represent the fact that your
redemption "out of Egypt" has changed the things you think. "That
the Lord's law may be in thy mouth: for with a strong hand hath
He brought thee out of Egypt" — it is to represent the fact that
not only has your redemption changed the things you do and
changed the things you think, but it has changed the things you

say! In other words, it is to represent a complete, revolutionary change of character and conduct. That was to be the significance of the Passover.

It would, therefore, be interesting to examine what they *did* in the wilderness, what they *thought* in the wilderness, and what they *said* in the wilderness!

WHAT THEY DID

Deuteronomy 12:1 — "These are the statutes and judgments, which ye shall observe to do in the land which the Lord God of thy fathers giveth thee to possess it, all the days that ye live upon the earth." Notice that they are to enjoy the land and possess it all the days that they are *on the earth* — not in heaven! Verse 7 — "And there ye shall eat before the Lord your God, and ye shall rejoice in all that ye put your hand unto, ye and your households, wherein the Lord thy God hath blessed thee." Everything you do will be a sheer delight! The whole of your activity will be bathed in joy! "Ye shall not do after all the things that we do here this day, every man whatsoever is right in his own eyes." That is what they were doing in the wilderness! Every man did whatsoever was *right in his own eyes.*

There was no sense of the sovereignty of God. Every man did what was right *in his own eyes.* His conduct was controlled by his own sincere convictions, maybe, but he knew nothing of the supreme direction of God in his soul.

A man in the wilderness, even though prompted by sincere motives, is subject to certain patterns of conduct to which he seeks to conform. His Christian activity and his Christian walk tend to be a drudgery rather than that sheer, pure joy that God purposes for His redeemed people, walking in the power and fulness and energy of God the Holy Spirit. Verse 9 — "For ye are not as yet come to the rest and the inheritance which the Lord your God giveth you."

While you are still doing what is right in your own eyes, you have not entered into rest, nor your inheritance. Hebrews 4:9, 10 — "There remaineth therefore a rest to the people of God. For he that is entered into his rest, he also hath ceased from his own works" — he has relinquished the right to do what is right in his own eyes and has submitted himself to the totalitarian dictatorship of Jesus Christ. He recognizes only that activity to be valid which stems from Him — which stems from the indwelling sovereignty of Jesus Christ, to whom he is sold out completely. This is the definition which God gives us of true spiritual rest.

What have *you* been *doing* since your redemption? Still what is right in your own eyes? Are you sold out for Jesus Christ? Do you still claim the right to choose your own career? You do not have that right! Do you still claim the right to choose the wife or husband you will marry? You do not have that right! Do you still claim the right to use your leisure hours as you please? You do not have that right! Do you still claim the right to spend your money as you please? You do not have that right! Do you still consider that you have the right to choose where you will spend your vacation? You do not have that right! Except in the wilderness!

Maybe that is precisely where you are right now — doing still what *you think* is right *in your own eyes,* because when you were redeemed by the blood of Jesus Christ and God once and for all forgave you, you never realized that this experience of Jesus Christ was a *crisis* calculated, in God's economy of things, to precipitate a *process,* a walk no longer under the dictates of the flesh, however sincere, but under the dictates of the Spirit. "For as many as are led by the Spirit of God, they are the children of God" (Romans 8:14).

The moment a man, woman, boy, or girl gives to the Holy Spirit the right to re-establish the sovereignty of Jesus Christ within his soul, he does not even have the right to do what is *right* in his own eyes — let alone what is *wrong!*

What They Thought

Now what did they think about in the wilderness? For this was to be "a memorial between their eyes" to indicate that all their thinking had been changed. What did they think about in the wilderness? Numbers 11:4-8 — "And the mixt multitude that was among them fell a lusting; and the children of Israel also wept again, and said, Who shall give us flesh to eat? We remember the fish, which we did eat in Egypt freely; the cucumbers, and the melons, and the leeks, and the onions, and the garlick; but now our soul is dried away: and there is nothing at all, beside this manna, before our eyes. And the manna was as coriander seed . . . . and the taste of it was as the taste of fresh oil."

Oil in the Bible is a beautiful picture of the Holy Spirit and, as we shall see more fully in a later chapter, the daily manna demonstrated constantly, supernaturally, the unrelenting presence of the living God in the midst of His redeemed people, but they got bored with it!

Nothing but manna! Manna for breakfast, manna for lunch, manna for supper, and manna for breakfast again — it gets a bit tedious after a bit, doesn't it? "Manna, manna, manna," they said, "seven days a week, fifty-two weeks in the year; manna, manna — we're sick and tired of manna!" But God never intended them to eat manna for forty years. God had prepared Canaan for them, but they stayed in the wilderness and dreamed of Egypt!

Maybe you say, "Oh, my Christian life is dull and boring to me. I read my Bible only out of a sense of duty." I tell you that if the Christian life has become dull and boring to you, it is simply because you will not go in to possess what God has given you in Jesus Christ. You have never tasted the thrill and adventure of being totally abandoned to the One who will lead you through in glory and in victory. I would not change places with you for a million dollars, if you *must* stick to manna for breakfast, manna for lunch, and manna for supper! It was good for the purpose for which it was given, but it was never intended to be their diet for forty years!

Here was a redeemed people, brought out of Egypt and on their way to the "land of promise," but with their thoughts, their ambitions, their appetites, fed by the memory of that from which God had redeemed them! "We remember the fish of Egypt; the cucumbers, and the melons, and the leeks, and the onions, and the garlick." Enslaved to the memories of that from which they had been redeemed! Their whole thought-life dominated by a defeated enemy whom God had buried to a man in the Red Sea, the place of death, into which, on the day of their redemption they, with Moses, had been baptized, to be raised miraculously by God and poised upon the threshold of a new walk that would lead them on and into a new land — the land to be possessed!

"The fish, the cucumbers, the melons, the leeks, the onions, and the garlick" — these were the things that occupied their minds in the wilderness! "We remember, we remember. . . " they said — and with what did they remember? With their minds! In their imagination they were still living in Egypt!

What is it that preoccupies your imagination as a redeemed sinner? With what does your mind busy itself? What are your ambitions? What are your appetites? Where do you go, what company do you keep and what do you do, in your mind? Have you been weaned from the things of Egypt?

Fish! Fish in a hot climate! Something particularly unsavoury! Cucumbers! Twelve inches of indigestion! Then the melons! Ninety-five per cent water and five per cent pips! And the onions and the garlick — things which speak for themselves!

It was with *these* things that they occupied their minds. With what do you occupy *your* mind? What is it that has captured the imagination of your heart since you were redeemed?

Sin is conceived in the imagination. First there comes the suggestion — the Satanic suggestion — and that suggestion becomes a desire; and if it is allowed to conceive and mature and be brought to birth within the area of your imagination, the desire will become an intent. It is at the point where desire becomes intent that you have already sinned, whether your circumstances allow you to implement your intent or not. That is why the Lord Jesus Christ said: ". . . whosoever looketh on a woman to lust after her hath committed adultery with her already in his heart" (Matthew 5:28).

Where suggestion becomes desire, desire becomes intent, and the intent becomes an act — the act becomes a memory and that memory is hung like a picture upon the wall of your imagination, in the picture gallery of your mind. When later in your thoughts you wander through the picture gallery, you see the memory on the wall, and this memory itself becomes a suggestion, and this suggestion becomes desire, and this desire may become intent; and if this intent becomes an act, you will then have hanging on the wall *two* memories, and the process can begin all over again with double force!

Do you see the principle? That is why every time you commit sin, you make it easier to commit another sin, because every time you commit sin, you are making "an altar to sin" (Hosea 8:11). Every sinful memory stimulates sinful desire, encourages sinful intent, and another sinful act which will become yet another sinful memory, until your mind is polluted.

Now we know what they were thinking about in the wilderness. They only had memories of that *from* which they had been redeemed, because they had never gone on and in, and so had no memories of that *to* which they had been redeemed.

What memories had they of Canaan in the wilderness? None! They had only heard sermons *about* Canaan! They only had secondhand talk about Canaan! They had no personal, vital, individual experience of Canaan; it was language, but not life, and nature abhors a vacuum!

I want to tell you this, that if you do not walk in the power of God the Holy Spirit, if your life is not abandoned to the indwelling sovereignty of Jesus Christ, then all the promises of victory in the Bible, all the promises of power by the Holy Spirit and of divine vocation will simply be texts, printed on so much paper — impersonal and irrelevant! Your mind will be filled only with memories of that which has been true to your experience in the bitterness of defeat.

No wonder they had nothing to celebrate in the wilderness!

WHAT THEY SAID

What did they say in the wilderness? This people who knew nothing of the sovereignty of God in their lives, to whom God gave such unrelenting evidence of His presence by the daily manna, but who never acted as though He mattered, who had received such lavish promises of a land to be possessed, yet could feed only upon their miserable memories of the past — what did this people have to say?

Numbers 16:3 — "They gathered themselves together

against Moses and against Aaron, and said unto them, Ye take too much upon you, seeing all the congregation are holy, every one of them, and the Lord is among them: wherefore then lift ye up yourselves above the congregation of the Lord?" That is what they said in the wilderness! They had become acclimatized to their circumstances in the desert and resisted any suggestion that their unhappy lot could be bettered in "the land." In their own estimation, they were all holy, "every one of them!" How holy? Holy enough!

How holy are you? Holy enough?

Nursing memories of Egypt, are you perfectly content to call yourself converted? Recognizing the witness of God's Spirit to your spirit that a wonderful thing has happened, you can remember the day you were redeemed, and yet are you perfectly content to live a self-centered life that renounces and repudiates the Lordship of Christ? Are you holy *enough?*

They resented every suggestion on the part of Moses and Aaron that they were missing God's purpose for their lives, on the ground that they were holy enough — but by whose standards? God's, or their own?

Is that how holy you are? You can always be holy enough *by your own standards!* In the day that Moses came down from the mountain with the tables of stone in his hands, the law of righteousness inscribed by the finger of God, he found the people half drunken, half naked, dancing round the golden calf — a redeemed people! Holy *enough* by their *own* standards!

It may well be that as you began to read this book you were firmly convinced that you were holy enough — ready still to resist the idea that you should be anything other than what you already are. Then do not miss that purpose for which this message comes to you, for redemption is a "day to be remembered" in a "land to be possessed" — and only there have you the legitimate right to celebrate the fact that the blood of Jesus Christ was shed that you might have peace with God.

Would you like to pray?

Dear Lord Jesus Christ, I thank Thee for Thy Word, quick and powerful, and sharper than any two-edged sword, piercing to the dividing asunder of soul and spirit, laying bare the thoughts and the intents of the heart, opening up to the glare of Thy righteousness the picture gallery of the mind. I bow before Thee as one who is naked before the eyes of Him with whom I have to do.

All my wanderings in the wilderness have not passed unnoticed. Every secret thought of my mind as I have meditated upon the flesh pots of Egypt has been recorded in heaven. All my rebellious talk has been heard by God! I have despised my birthright and I have neglected so many tokens that Thou hast given me of my inheritance. I can look back to a history of failure and of superficial dedication, in which I have boosted up my self-importance, and bitterly complained at every demand that God has made upon me.

I am heartily sick of this imitation of the real thing — this counterfeit Christian life, and I do not want it any more! I want to get in as I once got out, and to have something to celebrate in the land!

I know that Thou art the living God in the midst of Thy people. Do Thou Thine ancient work in me, for Thy Name's sake. Amen.

Any Old Bush Will Do!

5

Any Old Bush Will Do!

By God's miraculous intervention, Moses had been saved as a little baby out of the bulrushes, but Moses did not have any say in that! The best he could do at that stage in his career was to squeak! God had foreshadowed these things.

Over four hundred years before, God had told Abraham that He was going to raise up a deliverer for His people and save them from the tyranny of a wicked Pharaoh, and now God's hour had struck.

Preserved from death, Moses was introduced by God's divine providence into Pharaoh's household, adopted by his daughter, and nourished as her own son. With all the privileges of royalty, he received a magnificent education. He was trained as a statesman, a soldier, and an administrator, and by the age of 40 he was a polished, scholarly man who could have taken his place in any society. In the words of Acts 7:20 and 22 — "He was exceeding fair. . . . And Moses was learned in all the wisdom of the Egyptians, and was mighty in words and in deeds."

This is the portrait that God gives us of the man in the prime of life, highly qualified and filled with a sense of urgency, yet in his humility seemingly indifferent to his own intellectual stature — poised, it would seem, upon the threshold of a brilliant career. In point of fact, he was a man only a few hours away from a tragic blunder that would bring to frustration all his noblest ambitions and make him useless to God or man for forty years in the backside of the desert.

Acts 7:23 — "And when he was full forty years old, it came into his heart to visit his brethren the children of Israel.

And seeing one of them suffer wrong, he defended him, and avenged him that was oppressed, and smote the Egyptian: for he supposed his brethren would have understood how that God by his hand would deliver them: but they understood not." On the basis of what he was, and on the basis of what he knew, Moses took it for granted that he would be accepted in the ministry for which he believed God had called him — ". . . he *supposed* his brethren would have understood . . . but they understood not." With a strong sense of mission, he was baffled at his own impotence!

Maybe this is the dilemma into which you too have fallen. You have felt the surge of holy ambition. Your heart has burned within you. You have dreamed dreams and seen visions, but only to awaken again and again to a dull sense of futility, as one who beats the air or builds castles in the sky.

We need to turn to the record itself to discover how Moses lost the way. Exodus 2:11 — "And it came to pass in those days, when Moses was grown, that he went out unto his brethren, and looked on their burdens: and he spied an Egyptian smiting an Hebrew, one of his brethren." You can imagine the natural impulse of a man moved with compassion for his own kith and kin. There was nothing evil, there was nothing implicitly sinful or wrong in the thoughts that filled his mind; that natural feeling of resentment against a tyrannical people, mercilessly whipping one of his own defenseless brethren — but it was just at that stage that he allowed sincerity and genuine compassion to rob him of his true vocation.

It says in verse 12, "And he looked this way and that way, and when he saw that there was no man, he slew the Egyptian, and hid him in the sand." The enormity of the need knocked him off balance, and in a false sense of dedication he committed himself to the task instead of to God — "He looked this way and that way . . . ." The one way he did not look was up! ". . . and when he saw that there was no *man*, he slew the Egyptian, ..." In his sensitivity to the presence of man, Moses became strangely insensitive to the presence of God. How easy it is for us to do just that, and relate our actions to the approval or disapproval of men. Are you "man-conscious" or "God-conscious"?

Had Moses been overwhelmingly confident that his actions merited God's complete approval, he would have been indifferent to other men's reactions — their opinions would have been irrelevant. Spiritual pioneers, consciously in the center of God's will, can afford to be lonely in the face of public opinion, whether it be Nehemiah building the wall, Peter taking the Gospel to the house of a Gentile, or Wilberforce and Livingstone campaigning for the abolition of slavery.

Paul loved to preface his epistles by introducing himself as "an apostle, (not of men, neither by man, but by Jesus Christ, and God the Father, who raised him from the dead)" (Galatians 1:1). Yes, ". . . by the will of God"! That was his mandate, that was all he needed to know, and so he could say, ". . . the Holy Ghost witnesseth in every city, saying that bonds and afflictions abide me. But none of these things move me, neither count I my life dear unto myself, so that I might finish my course with joy, and the ministry, which I have received of the Lord Jesus, to testify the gospel of the grace of God" (Acts 20:23, 24). He had become invulnerable; he had a God-given sense of vocation.

Moses lost his sense of God, and maybe you have lost your sense of God for the same reason. You are not called upon to commit yourself to a need, or to a task, or to a field. You are called upon to commit yourself to God! It is He then who takes care of the consequences and commits you where *He* wants you. He is the Lord of the harvest! He is the Head of the body — and He is gloriously competent to assume His own responsibilities! Man is not indispensable to God. God is indispensable to man!

I sometimes have an uneasy feeling about certain missionary conventions and the missionary challenge to which we have become accustomed. You hear one speaker after another committing you to the *task*, claiming your life for this mission field or for that. "The need," all too often it is said, "constitutes the call"! There are a *thousand* needs, but you are not committed to these. You are committed to Christ, and it is *His* business to commit you where He wants you. No man or woman on earth has the right to commit any member of the body of Jesus Christ to any task, or to any field; that is to usurp the authority of the Head of the body, Jesus Christ Himself. I Corinthians 12:18 — "But now hath God set the members every one of them in the body, as it hath pleased him." The moment I claim the right to commit a man or a woman or a boy or a girl to some field of service, I blaspheme His sovereign place as Lord of the harvest.

God is perfectly capable of taking care of His own affairs, and the reason so little is being accomplished by the Church of Jesus Christ today is that we have all too often organized God out of business. Millions of man hours and countless millions of dollars are being misspent on man's promotional activity, unasked, on God's behalf.

This is not to challenge the sincerity of those who are thus employed, but we so often confuse bustle for business, and plant for power, and perspiration for inspiration. What an embarrassment it would be to you if you had a pair of hands that always tried to demonstrate how busy they were! Do you expect your fingers to tell you each morning what their program is for the day, and then demonstrate their enthusiasm by a vigorous show of uncontrolled activity? Do you think you would be successful in playing the piano on that basis? I would not like to ask a barber who had hands like that to shave me!

Surely, what the head demands of every member of the body is *restful availability*, and prompt response to every impulse of the head in instant obedience, producing the co-ordinated activity of the whole, and the orderly fulfillment of that purpose to which each, as a member of the team, has been committed in particular.

The challenge we hear so often today in the name of consecration is "Do more! Give more! Be more!" Go! Go! Go! But God says, "Be *still*, and know that *I* am God"! In other words, quit the panic! Just let God be God!

Moses had not learned that lesson when he saw the Egyptian smiting one of his brethren. He rolled up his sleeves, and said in so many words, "If ever there was a time when I was on call, it is now!" and he blundered in like a bull in a china shop, smote the Egyptian, and tried unsuccessfully to bury him. With the best intentions in the world, he became a murderer instead of a missionary!

"And when he went out the second day, behold, two men of the Hebrews strove together: and he said to him that did the wrong, Wherefore smitest thou thy fellow? And he said, Who made thee a prince and a judge over us? intendest thou to kill me, as thou killedst the Egyptian? And Moses feared, and said, Surely this thing is known" (Exodus 2:13, 14). Yes, the thing was known. When Moses tried to tackle the job, he could not even bury one Egyptian successfully. Maybe he left his toes sticking out of the sand! When *God* tackled the job, He buried the whole lot of them in the Red Sea! That is how competent God is to deal with His own business.

Moses fled, for "when Pharaoh heard this thing, he sought to slay him" — and for forty years he was in the land of Midian. A man whom God had specifically raised up for a particular task, but who on the basis of his own sincerity, and on the basis of his own enthusiasm, neutralized his usefulness because he committed himself to a need instead of to God. He tried to do God's work man's way, and he had to learn that it is not scholarship but relationship — not just his *ability* but his *availability* — that qualifies a man for God.

One can imagine the awful sense of futility that must have overwhelmed Moses again and again during those forty years of uselessness, unrecognized and unknown in the backside of the desert, and maybe you too have found your Christian service unrewarding. You are converted, you can look back to the day when you put your trust in Jesus Christ as your personal Saviour, but you imagined that the Christian life was just conforming to certain patterns of Christian conduct — patterns which had been projected upon you — and that your spirituality would be judged in terms of your conformity. That is not spirituality, that is "copyism," and Christian service that stems solely from conformity to the demands of an organizational machine will always be lacking in spiritual luster, and characterized by the absence of divine unction. You will waste away with Moses in the wilderness of Midian.

Poor Moses — soldier, scholar, and statesman! Born to
be a leader, caring for a handful of sheep, his wife's husband,
with a job on her father's farm! Hope must have seemed to
wither at the roots, when "the angel of the Lord appeared unto
him in a flame of fire out of the midst of a bush; and he looked,
and, behold, the bush burned with fire, and the bush was not
consumed" (Exodus 3:2).

When Moses saw that bush, he was amazed! It was a
phenomenon — something that immediately attracted his attention. Here was a bush that burned and burned and burned, and
went on burning. As far as he could see, it could burn on for
eternity, and he could not help but compare himself with that
bush! In his heart he must have said something like this: "I
have never seen a bush like that before. I'm not like that bush!
Forty years ago I burned myself out in 24 hours, and I have
been a heap of ashes for forty years since. There must be something very unusual about that bush, something very unique!
It must be a very wonderful bush!" And Moses said, "I will
now turn aside and see this great sight, why the bush is not
burnt." Aroused within his heart there was a holy curiosity,
and he did a very wise thing — he made intelligent inquiry and,
in consequence, he made a very wonderful discovery!

So often there is aroused within us a holy curiosity, but
it is unmatched by intelligent inquiry, and that is why we do not
make the same wonderful discovery!

We are tutored in these days to hero worship. In every
walk of life we become "fans," and that is not less true in the
area of Christian activity. There are those in whose lives there
is manifestly evident the mighty unction and power of God.
They are transparently genuine. The hand of God is upon
them. They speak with an authority that God honors. Lives
are transformed. Those spiritually dead are raised to life again.
Defeated, helpless, useless, barren Christians are transformed
into useful vehicles of divine life. Wherever they go it seems
that there is a touch of glory about their path, and we admire
them and applaud — but we stand back as though this were
to be the monopoly of the few! As though they have a special
call upon the grace of God and as though this were something

not for the common run of men. We say in our hearts, "There is a bush that burns! I would like to be a bush like that, but I am just a heap of ashes!" — and that is as far as it gets.

You discuss the burning bush with others! You admit that it is an amazing thing, and maybe you invite others to come and look at the phenomenon, but you have resigned yourself to be nothing more than what you are — a heap of ashes! It has never dawned upon you that you could be anything different, so you have to make the best of a bad job in your own little desert! Resigned to sit on the balcony among the spectators, just to be average, a spiritual nonentity!

This is the attitude that Paul sought above everything else to avoid in those of whom it had been his privilege to lead to the Lord Jesus Christ. That is the significance of his words to the Philippians when he wrote, "Work out your own salvation with fear and trembling. For it is God that worketh in you both to will and to do of his good pleasure" (Philippians 2:12, 13).

To the Philippians, who were tempted to lean upon Paul as their spiritual crutch, as though God had a particular interest in him that He did not have in them, he said, in so many words, "All that God has given to me, He has given to you! The Lord Jesus Christ who dwells in my humanity is the same Lord Jesus Christ who dwells in your humanity. What I have, you have! What I can be by the grace of God, you can be by the grace of God! Work out your own salvation! It is yours as much as mine. It is God, not Paul the apostle, who works in you, both to will and to do of His good pleasure. Recognize that all the illimitable resources that God has vested in me in the Person of His own dear Son are the same illimitable resources that He has vested in you!"

This is the message of the Bible, that God has chosen the weak and the base and the nothing, and the things that are not, to confound the things that are, and all God demands of a man is his availability — to be what man was created to be, the human vehicle of the divine life, inhabited by God for God. That God may be Himself — His size in terms of what you are on earth, in your availability to Him. What you are is totally irrelevant — nationality-wise, money-wise, education-wise, personality-wise, and any other wise, if only you will recognize the principle that it is God that works in you, to will and to do of His good pleasure.

The only ultimate source of divine activity in all spiritual life is God Himself — "Christ in you the hope of glory" (Colossians 1:27). The Church is so slow to learn. It admires and seeks to emulate the example of the mighty, but so seldom takes the trouble "to turn aside and see" the reason why. You read the lives of men like Hudson Taylor, George Mueller, Dwight L. Moody, A. B. Simpson — men whose lives have made spiritual history. You would like to be like them and do the things they did, and yet maybe you have never taken the trouble to find out *why* it was they were what they were, nor *how* it was they did what they did! Instead, you mobilize your own resources and seek to emulate the example they set, and are constantly buffeted by a sense of frustration because of your hopeless failure in the endeavor.

As some have sought to introduce you to the principle that made these men what they were, and enabled them to do what they did, you have been impatient, and said, "Don't interfere! I'm too busy trying to be like them, and I don't have time to listen to you!" Now is that not stupid? Why was Hudson Taylor what he was, and how could he do what he did? Why was A. B. Simpson what *he* was, and how could he do what *he* did? Were they God's favorites? Of course they were not! They were simply men who had qualified in the school of failure and despair. They were men who came to the end of themselves and discovered that what they were apart from God was nothing!

Moses began by being a failure! That was the school from which he qualified! Abraham began by being a failure! That was the school from which *he* qualified! Jacob was a hopeless failure! David was a hopeless failure! Elijah was a hopeless failure! Isaiah was a hopeless failure and a "man of unclean lips," but it is in the school of destitution — the bitter school of self-discovery — that finally you graduate into usefulness, when at last you discover the total bankruptcy of what you are apart from what God is! These men made this discovery, and were blessed!

Moses had to discover this, and you will have to discover it! He had to discover that a fine physique and noble ambitions, royal breeding and Egyptian scholarship, could never be a substitute for that for which man was created — God Himself!

Moses said, "I will now turn aside and see this great sight, why the bush is not burnt. And when the Lord saw that he turned aside to see, God called unto him out of the midst of the bush, and said, Moses, Moses." God called him by name! *When* did God call him? While he stood admiring at a distance? No, God never said a word then — but "when he turned aside to see," God called!

Maybe you are wondering why it is that you have never had an urgent sense of call; why in your Christian life there is no real driving sense of direction; why you do not have a deep spirit-born conviction of the purpose for which you have been redeemed; why it is you drift, and live with no target in view! Maybe it is because you never took time out to find the reason why! When Moses turned aside to see, God called him — by name!

Judged by purely human standards, you may be highly qualified for Christian service, and yet go out into the oblivion of spiritual uselessness. No matter to what distinction you may attain in this world, no matter how much you may be acclaimed by your fellow men, no matter how gifted you may be, it is tragically possible for you to go down in the annals of spiritual history as one of those who did not count, either for God or man — and do you know why? Because you never took time out to find the reason why God uses men! You have been too busy, and you never turned aside to see, and God was silent. He never called you by your name!

And as God called, Moses said, "Here am I. And (God) said, Draw not nigh hither: put off thy shoes from off thy feet, for the place whereon thou standest is holy ground. Moreover he said, I am the God of thy father, the God of Abraham, the God of Isaac, and the God of Jacob. And Moses hid his face; for he was afraid to look upon God" (Exodus 3:4-6). God had something to say to Moses, and I think that it must have been something like this: "Moses, you have done a wise thing in making intelligent inquiry, for you thought that this was a very remarkable bush. You thought that there must be something about it at once peculiar and wonderful, something unique, that it could burn and burn and burn, and go on burning, and yet not burn itself out. But you are wrong — you are *quite* wrong! Do you see that bush over there? That scruffy, scraggy looking thing — *that* bush would have done! Do you see this beautiful looking bush, so shapely and fine — *this* bush would have done! For you see, Moses, *any old bush* will do — *any* old bush — if only *God* is in the bush! The trouble with you, Moses, is this: forty years ago, learned in all the wisdom of the Egyptians, mighty in word and deed, you admired your own foliage! You thought you were some bush! But you burned yourself out in 24 hours, and you have been a heap of ashes for forty years! If this bush that you have admired were depending upon its own substance to sustain the flame, it too would burn itself out in 24 hours; it too would be a heap of ashes like you. But it is not the *bush* that sustains the flame, it is God *in* the bush; and *any old bush* will do!"

Did you ever make this discovery? Have you ever come to the place where you realized that all you can produce, at your best, is ashes? Did you ever come to the place where you presented yourself for what you are — *nothing* — to be filled with what He is — *everything* — and to step out into every new day, conscious that the eternal I AM is all you need, for all His will!

This is the forgotten tense of the Church of Jesus Christ today. We live either in the *past* tense or in the *future* tense. We say either "Ebenezer — hitherto hath the Lord helped us," or we comfort ourselves with "Maranatha — Behold the Lord cometh," — but we forget that He is the eternal I AM, the eternal *present* tense, adequate right *now* for every need!

If you are born again, all you need is *what you have,* and what you have is *what He is!* He does not *give* you strength — He *is* your strength! He does not give you victory — He *is* your victory!

Do you understand the principle? Christ is in you —

nothing less than that! You cannot have *more,* and you do not need to have *less,* and every day can be the glorious fulfillment of the divine end — "Proving what is that good, and acceptable, and perfect, will of God," as you present your body a living sacrifice, holy and acceptable unto God, which is your reasonable service.

Only remember this — any old bush will do!

The Church in the Wilderness

6

The Church in the Wilderness

IT IS PLAINLY INDICATED TO US IN THE BIBLE THAT THE EARTHLY
Israel and God's dealings with them are a picture of a greater
spiritual Israel, ". . . For they are not all Israel, which are of
Israel: neither, because they are the seed of Abraham, are they
all children: but, In Isaac shall thy seed be called. That is,
They which are the children of the flesh, these are not the children of God: but the children of the promise are counted for
the seed" (Romans 9:6-8).

Paul, in this passage, is simply stating the fact that it is
not their natural affiliation to Israel that makes them the true
Israel of God, but faith that appropriates the promise of redemption. "For he is not a Jew, which is one outwardly; neither is
that circumcision, which is outward in the flesh: but he is a
Jew, which is one inwardly, and circumcision is that of the
heart, in the spirit, and not in the letter; whose praise is not of
men, but of God" (Romans 2:28, 29). It is to this spiritual
significance of circumcision to which Paul refers again in Colossians 2:11 when he writes, "In whom also we are circumcised
with the circumcision made without hands, in putting off the
body of the sins of the flesh by the circumcision of Christ:
buried with him in baptism, wherein also ye are risen with him
through the faith of the operation of God, who hath raised him
from the dead." Here, this circumcision made without hands in
the experience of the spiritual Israel of God is representative of
the believer's identity with the Lord Jesus in His death and
resurrection, and this of course is fully in keeping with the vivid
picture that God gives us in the historical record of the earthly
Israel.

God made a covenant with Abraham in Genesis 17:8, 10, 11 — "And I will give unto thee, and to thy seed after thee, the land wherein thou art a stranger, all the land of Canaan, for an everlasting possession; and I will be their God. . . . Every man child among you shall be circumcised. . . . and it shall be a token of the covenant betwixt me and you." Circumcision was to be the hallmark of a redeemed people destined for the plenitude of Canaan, and yet in Joshua 5:5 we read that "all the people that were born in the wilderness by the way as they came forth out of Egypt, them they had not circumcised." For this was the Church in the Wilderness, a people who had come out, but who had not gone in — dumped in the desert! Circumcision in Egypt was a confession of faith, but circumcision in the wilderness could only have been a confession of failure.

In the picture language of the Bible, they had gone through all the motions, but in common with all too much of Christendom today, they had "a form of godliness, but denying the power thereof" (II Timothy 3:5).

All had been "baptized unto Moses in the cloud and in the sea" (I Corinthians 10:2) and one might almost describe Moses as pastor of the First Baptist Church in the Wilderness! We have seen already in an earlier chapter that as they were baptized into Moses, so we have been baptized into Christ. They went with him into the place of death, to be raised with him into newness of life on the other side of the Red Sea. In God's purpose we too have gone with Christ into the place of death, to be raised with Him into newness of life — "For by the death He died He died to sin [ending His relation to it] once for all, and the life that He lives He is living to God — in unbroken fellowship with Him. Even so consider yourselves also dead to sin *and* your relation to it broken, but [that you are] alive to God — living in unbroken fellowship with Him — in Christ Jesus" (Romans 6:10, 11 *Amplified New Testament*).

This is your spiritual baptism into Christ. It is quite obvious that you can be baptized outwardly without being baptized inwardly. Baptism cannot make us true Christians. If there is no spiritual content to the outward exercise, baptism becomes no more than an empty superstition. That, of course, is obvious, and there is only spiritual content where *faith* has been exercised, in *obedience* to the truth.

Not only were they baptized into Moses, however, but they "did all eat the same spiritual meat; and did all drink the same spiritual drink: for they drank of that spiritual Rock that followed them: and that Rock was Christ" (I Corinthians 10:3, 4).

We have also touched upon the spiritual significance of the manna — the "spiritual meat" upon which, the Church in the Wilderness fed throughout their forty weary years of wandering, but I would like to examine this now a little more closely.

"And when the children of Israel saw it, they said one to another, It is manna." What the children of Israel said when they saw the manna may be translated — "What is this?" for ". . . they wist not what it was" (Exodus 16:15). This was something new, something that they had never tasted before; it was God's gift to a redeemed people, and it represents for you and for me the gift of God's Holy Spirit, to those who have been redeemed in the precious blood of Christ.

No man, woman, or child can ever receive, taste, or know this heavenly gift until he has put his trust in Christ "in whom also," wrote Paul to the Ephesians, "after that ye believed, ye were sealed with that holy Spirit of promise, which is the earnest of our inheritance . . ." (Ephesians 1:13, 14), and of whom the Lord Jesus said, "even the Spirit of truth; whom the world cannot receive, because it seeth him not, neither knoweth him: but ye know him; for he dwelleth with you, and shall be in you" (John 14:17). The presence of the Holy Spirit is the birthright of forgiven sinners, and the miracle of regeneration is a new and novel experience, introducing the newborn child of God into a quality of life of which, until then, he has lived in total ignorance.

The taste of the manna was "as the taste of fresh oil" (Numbers 11:8), speaking, as we have already mentioned, of the presence of the Holy Spirit, and yet the role played by the manna in the Church in the Wilderness was not representative of His full, gracious ministry. It was but a foretaste of better things to come! It is significant that in Exodus 16:31 we read that "the taste of it was like wafers made with honey." Oil and honey! The Holy Spirit, reminding God's people of a day to be remembered in a land to be possessed! Not just a dry thin wafer, but a *land* flowing with milk and honey! There is not much substance in a wafer — just enough to stimulate the salivary juices and make the hungry cry for more!

The two-fold taste of the manna speaks of the dual role of the Holy Spirit in the Church in the Wilderness. The taste of oil speaks of His witness to the presence of the living God in the human spirit of the forgiven sinner, and the taste of honey speaks of His constant incentive to the wilderness Christian to get on and get in, to live in the land, to be filled with the Spirit.

I am fully aware that very often the daily manna is used as a picture of your daily Bible reading, and it makes quite a good picture in that they went out every morning and they gathered. However, the more they gathered of it, the more they got sick of it, and complained, "But now our soul is dried away: there is nothing at all, beside this manna, before our eyes" (Numbers 11:6). It had become dull and monotonous and boring. Should this be true of your daily Bible reading?

I cannot feel that this picture presents a very happy precedent, and I am sure that we should not accept it as the norm of Christian experience. Your daily Bible reading is designed to allow the Holy Spirit to lead you into all truth, so that you may increasingly ". . . become a body wholly filled and flooded with God Himself!" (Ephesians 3:19 *Amplified New Testament*). It is designed to show you the wealth and heritage that is yours in Christ, but the more *they* had of manna, day after day, week after week, month after month, year after year, the more they disliked it!

Mind you, even in relation to your daily Bible reading, this could be equally true of you! If you will not respond to the Holy Spirit and the incentive that He constantly gives you through His Word to holiness of life, nor be enticed by the taste of the honey, then the wafer will remain stubbornly thin, and dry, and uninteresting — and your quiet time will degenerate into a mechanical performance that may conform to pattern, but provide you with little pleasure or profit. You *may* be sustained, but you will hardly be satisfied!

The witness of the Spirit to the redeemed sinner living in disobedience is an extremely unpleasant experience, and for the Christian who gets out but who refuses to get in, the things of the Spirit will become increasingly monotonous. The pastor in the pulpit, the missionary on the field, the teacher in his Bible class, who belong to the Church in the Wilderness, and who by force of circumstance must go on going through the motions of Christian service, will become increasingly bored in all they do, and become increasingly boring to those for whom they do it!

That is why there are so many boring preachers and boring Sunday school teachers. They are as boring as they are bored themselves!

There were some who belonged to the Church in the Wilderness who were living in willful rebellion and disobedience; they would gladly have escaped any conscious sense of God's presence, for it constantly reminded them that they were a redeemed people. To such the daily witness of the manna was, paradoxically enough, at one and the same time both a source of aggravation and of relief. On the one hand it disturbed a conscience already ill at ease, and yet upon the other they were strangely aware that they could not live without it! They were spoiled for Egypt, and were not enjoying Canaan! This is the paradox of the carnal Christian.

Perhaps you, too, with them and with Jonah of old, have been trying to run away from God — and yet you cannot! You resist His claims, and yet are fearful lest He should forsake you! You are still a soul in conflict — you belong to the Church in the Wilderness!

But if the daily presence of the manna was a source of discomfort to some, it was a source of untold comfort to others!

Caleb and Joshua were men who never ceased to believe

that the God who brought them out was the God who could bring them in, and I sometimes feel that when they saw the wickedness, and the idolatry, and the grumbling, and the unbelief of God's people in the wilderness, they must have turned to each other and said, "God will leave us! God *must* leave us!" Then through the long watches of a restless night, they would wait fearfully for the dawn, to see if God had left them! At the first hint of daylight they would scan the ground at their feet, and would see the manna, and would be comforted! God had not left them — there was His witness!

While Moses was away in the mountain speaking with God and receiving the law, Aaron yielded to the pressure of the people and, half naked in their shame, they worshiped the golden calf which he had made. What despair and what misgivings must have filled the hearts of the faithful few, and yet the next morning, mingled with the shattered fragments of those tables of stone, which had been written upon with the finger of God — there was manna on the ground! This is the amazing patience of God! This is a love that will not let you go! ". . . where sin abounded, grace did much more abound" (Romans 5:20), and God has said, "I will never leave you, nor forsake you" (Hebrews 13:5).

There is no mandate here for disobedience, nor does it make sin less serious, but I want you to know that when all seems lost, mercy can shine through judgment, and the rainbow of God's promise tells of One who "shall not fail nor *be discouraged,* till he have set judgment in the earth" (Isaiah 42:4). When every hope is dashed, when every noble dream and every holy ambition written with the finger of God Himself upon your heart is shattered, hope can rise again, and grace can chase away the gloom — *there is manna on the ground!* He has not left you — nor left you comfortless! Then "grieve not the holy Spirit of God, whereby ye are sealed unto the day of redemption" (Ephesians 4:30).

To the prophet Haggai (chapter 2 verse 5), God said, "According to the word that I covenanted with you when ye came out of Egypt, so my spirit remaineth among you: fear ye not." God might well have said to His people of old, "For forty years you grieved my Spirit, and yet I never left you! I never left you!" The daily manna tells us of a Holy Spirit who seals us until the day of redemption. You may grieve Him, you may quench Him, and if you do, He will let you know it—for "whom the Lord loveth He chasteneth"—but He will never leave you! This is the amazing grace of God!

However, while God was *feeding* His people in the wilderness—He let them *hunger.* Deuteronomy 8:2, 3—"And thou shalt remember all the way which the Lord thy God led thee these forty years in the wilderness, to humble thee, and to prove thee, to know what was in thine heart, whether thou wouldest keep his commandments, or no. And he humbled thee, and suffered thee to hunger, and fed thee with manna...." All those forty years, in other words, they were never satisfied, for the manna was given only to sustain life, but never to satisfy, because God never *intended* them to be satisfied in the wilderness!

Where did God intend to satisfy His people? In the land! God refuses to satisfy His people in the wilderness, when He has spread the table with good things in Canaan!

God will never satisfy *you* in the wilderness. You are no good to anybody in the wilderness! Basically you will never change in the wilderness! There will be no glow to your testimony, and the first enthusiasm of Christian service, the novelty of being on the mission field, of being the pastor of a church, or teaching a Bible class in Sunday school, will soon wear off when you get accustomed to the new sights and sounds and the people you have to live with in the wilderness. The vision will grow dim, and the light of battle will vanish from your eyes, and ignoring what you *need,* you will begin to clamor for what you *want,* and if you are not careful—God will give it to you!

The people "lusted exceedingly in the wilderness, and tempted God in the desert. And He gave them their request; but sent leanness unto their soul" (Psalm 106:14, 15). The quails God sent them rotted in their mouths, and they lived in self-imposed poverty, carnally fat and spiritually thin!

It is a sad thing to be impoverished by the things you *want*, while God is waiting to give you the things you *need*. Hezekiah clamored for another fifteen years of life, and he got what he wanted! But he "rendered not again according to the benefit done unto him; for his heart was lifted up: therefore there was wrath upon him . . ." (II Chronicles 32:25). He lived to beget one of the wickedest kings who ever reigned over Judah — Manasseh, who was 12 years old when Hezekiah died 15 years too late! Manasseh "built again the high places which Hezekiah his father had broken down. . . . and made Judah and the inhabitants of Jerusalem to err, and to do worse than the heathen, whom the Lord had destroyed before the children of Israel (II Chronicles 33:3, 9). What a pity Hezekiah did not die on schedule! He got what he wanted, *and died too old!*

No, the Church in the Wilderness was not a happy church — but what a transformation on the day they got into the land! Joshua 5:10 — "And the children of Israel encamped in Gilgal, and kept the passover on the fourteenth day of the month at even in the plains of Jericho." The first time for thirty-eight years! "And they did eat of the old corn of the land on the morrow after the passover, unleavened cakes, and parched corn in the selfsame day. And the manna ceased on the morrow after they had eaten of the old corn of the land; neither had the children of Israel manna any more; but they did eat of the fruit of the land of Canaan that year." For the bare *witness* of the Spirit, now they enjoyed the *fulness* of the Spirit. Not just sustained — now they were satisfied! Not just the thin, dry wafer — a foretaste of good things to come — but the *land itself* flowing with milk and honey; and for the monotonous diet of the desert, they had all the abundance of Canaan!

Are you bored? Are you suffering from leanness of soul? Have the things of God become monotonous? Are you more tempted to grumble than rejoice? Are the things you want more important than the things you need? Are you spiritually thin? Perhaps you are still living on manna! Maybe you got out but you never got in! Maybe you still belong to the Church in the Wilderness!

Oh, our God, may we enter increasingly into the good

of Thy rich provision, that the memories of Canaan may soon banish the memories of Egypt, and the fulness of Thy Spirit flood our souls with the light of the knowledge of the glory of God in the face of Jesus Christ. Every horizon beckons us, bright with the promise of Thy blessing; we must and we will go on and in, to explore and to possess the land! In Jesus' Name. Amen.

Then Came Amalek!

7

Then Came Amalek!

IN THE PRECEDING CHAPTER WE HAVE SEEN SOMETHING OF THE significance of the manna, and we need now to turn for a moment to Exodus 17, that we may understand to what Paul referred when he wrote in I Corinthians 10, not only of the "spiritual meat" (verse 3), but also of "the same spiritual drink: for they drank of that spiritual Rock that followed them: and that Rock was Christ" (verse 4).

As the children of Israel journeyed from the Wilderness of Sin, to pitch their tents in Rephidim, there was no water for the people to drink, and as became increasingly their characteristic in the wilderness, the people murmured against Moses and chided with him, and "Moses cried unto the Lord, saying, What shall I do unto this people? they be almost ready to stone me" (Exodus 17:4). In answer to his cry, God told Moses to take the rod in his hand, with which he smote the river, and said, "Behold, I will stand before thee there upon the rock in Horeb; and thou shalt smite the rock, and there shall come water out of it, that the people may drink (17:6). This Moses did, and water flowed from the smitten rock. The people drank and their thirst was quenched.

The picture here is clear. Water from the smitten rock in a thirsty land represents the gift of eternal life through the crucified Lord Jesus Christ, for in the words of Paul, the apostle, "that Rock was Christ."

As we shall discover later, this does not tell the whole of the story, but it does represent its beginning, for here indeed is the only place where the story of man's redemption can begin — at the place where the Rock was smitten.

Beneath the cross of Jesus
I fain would take my stand,
The shadow of a mighty rock,
Within a weary land;
A home within the wilderness,
A rest upon the way,
From the burning of the noontide heat,
And the burden of the day.

O safe and happy shelter!
O refuge tried and sweet!
O trysting-place where heaven's love
And heaven's justice meet!
As to the holy patriarch
That wondrous dream was given,
So seems my Saviour's cross to me,
A ladder up to heaven

Here then is the threefold portrait which God gives of a redeemed people living in the wilderness: They were baptized unto Moses — the believer identified with Christ and taken with Him through death into resurrection life. They were partakers of the daily manna — the believer experiencing the *witness* of the Holy Spirit to his heart, that he is a child of God, sealed unto the day of redemption, but having only a foretaste of all that Christ can be to those who enjoy the *fulness* of His Spirit. They were refreshed with water from the smitten rock — the believer receiving the gift of eternal life, on the basis of redemption through the precious blood of the crucified Lord Jesus Christ. But in spite of all this, ". . . with many of them God was not well pleased."

Returning to Exodus 17, we see that no sooner had God given water to this people from the rock that Moses smote than "then came Amalek and fought with Israel in Rephidim." Amalek here is a picture of the flesh, seeking at all costs to bar the onward journey of God's redeemed people, through the wilderness, into the Land of Promise.

It was not God's purpose that His people should remain at the place where the rock was smitten. Moses reminded Israel in Deuteronomy 1:6 — "The Lord our God spake unto us in Horeb, saying, Ye have dwelt long enough in this mount." How long had they dwelt in the Mount in Horeb? Long enough! "Turn you, and take your journey and go . . . Behold, I have set the land before you: go in and possess the land which the Lord sware unto your fathers, Abraham, Isaac, and Jacob, to give unto them and to their seed after them" (verses 7 and 8). In other words, "Get down, get on, and get in!" But this, it was Amalek's business and ambition to prevent!

Amalek presents us with a most fascinating study, and illustrates the relentless consistency of the Holy Spirit in the language which He uses in His revelation of truth throughout the whole of the Bible. He may use several types or symbols to illustrate the same spiritual principle, but such types or symbols as He may choose, He will use with complete consistency throughout the whole of Scripture.

This is one of the most remarkable evidences of the miraculous inspiration of the Bible. You will discover that the Bible will come to life in a new way, and the Old Testament in particular will become very much richer, a Book charged with spiritual significance, if you will allow the Holy Spirit to teach you the meaning of the language that He uses.

We have already seen that just as soon as the Holy Spirit is restored to your human spirit as a forgiven sinner, His office is to re-invade your soul, there to re-establish the sovereignty of the Lord Jesus in the area of your mind, of your emotions, and of your will — so that your whole human personality may become available to Him, who has come to re-inhabit your redeemed humanity, and that your body might become the temple of the living God.

There is, however, immediate resistance on the part of the flesh, "For the flesh lusteth against the Spirit and the Spirit against the flesh" (Galatians 5:17). The flesh contests every attempt of the Spirit of God to lead you on into spiritual maturity. Standing across your pathway from the very outset of your Christian life is Amalek!

And Moses said unto Joshua, Choose out men and go out, fight with Amalek: Tomorrow I will stand on the top of the hill with the rod of God in mine hand. So Joshua did as Moses had said to him, and fought with Amalek (Exodus 17:9, 10).

So Joshua was on the battlefield, and Joshua engaged the enemy; yet the outcome of the battle did not rest with him, for ". . . when Moses held up his hand, Israel prevailed; and when he let down his hand, Amalek prevailed." The principle is plain. Victory over Amalek is God given; it cannot be *won*, it can only be *received*, and that by the appropriation of faith.

In Exodus 4, we see that after God commissioned Moses to be the means in His hands of bringing His people out of Egypt, Moses answered and said,

> Behold, they will not believe me, nor hearken unto my voice: for they will say, The Lord hath not appeared unto thee. And the Lord said unto him, What is that in thine hand? And he said, A rod. And He said, Cast it on the ground. And he cast it on the ground, and it became a serpent; and Moses fled from before it. And the Lord said unto Moses, Put forth thine hand, and take it by the tail. And he put forth his hand, and caught it, and it became a rod in his hand (verses 1-4).

This was the sign that God gave to Moses of a victory already won, a victory that God gives to those who trust Him. As he fled before the serpent, God said in so many words, "Don't run away from it! Turn round! Face it! Put out your hand and take it by the tail!" — and the moment Moses put out his hand and took it, the serpent became as helpless and harmless as a rod.

What is the serpent in your life before which you have been fleeing? As a Christian, what is it that has been chasing you? Of what are you afraid? God says, "Stop running away — there is victory for you too! Turn round, put out your hand, and *take* the victory that I will give you!" When Moses let his hand down, Amalek prevailed, and Joshua was fighting a battle already lost. When Moses held his hand high, Joshua prevailed — and he enjoyed the victory already won!

There are countless Christians fighting a battle that is already lost, trying in their own strength to overcome the subtleties of sin. That is a battle you can fight all your days, but I tell you now, you cannot win! It is a battle already lost, lost in the first Adam, who was made a living soul, and died; but the last Adam, Jesus Christ, has already defeated sin and death and hell, and Satan himself! Why not accept in Him the victory that He has already won? Victory over the flesh is not to be attained — it is to be received.

"Walk in the Spirit, and you will not fulfil the lusts of the flesh" (Galatians 5:16). No matter what it is that threatens you, if you walk in the Spirit, you can turn around and face

your enemy. You can "take him by the tail" and find him helpless and harmless in your hands, for God has already bruised the
serpent's head! (Genesis 3:15; Hebrews 2:14). In other words,
to walk in the Spirit is to *assume* by faith the victory with which
He credits you, and God will vindicate your assumption, and
make it real in your experience.

Now the devil loves to invert truth and turn it into a
lie, and probably what he has been saying to you is this: "Try
not to fulfil the lusts of the flesh, and *then* you will walk in the
Spirit," as though the latter were a reward for the former. He
knows that in this way, he will keep you preoccupied with yourself, instead of being preoccupied with Christ.

There is nothing quite so nauseating or pathetic as the
flesh trying to be holy! The flesh has a perverted bent for
righteousness — but such righteousness as it may achieve is
always self-righteousness; and self-righteousness is always self-
conscious righteousness; and self-conscious righteousness is always full of self-praise. This produces the extrovert, who must
always be noticed, recognized, consulted, and applauded. On
the other hand, when the flesh in pursuit of self-righteousness
fails, instead of being filled with self-praise, it is filled with self-
pity, and this produces the introvert. A professional "case" for
professional counsellors!

The devil does not mind whether you are an extrovert
or an introvert, whether you succeed or whether you fail in the
energy of the flesh, whether you are filled with self-pity or self-
praise, for he knows that in both cases you will be preoccupied
with yourself, and not with Christ. You will be "ego-centric" —
self-centered — and not "Deo-centric" — God-centered!

So Satan will seek to persuade you that "walking in the
Spirit" is simply the *consequence* of your pious endeavor not to
fulfill the "lusts of the flesh," of which he himself is the author,
and thus by subtly confusing the means for the end, he will rob
you of what he knows to be your only possibility of victory.

Is that not what you have been trying to do? You have
been trying not to fulfill the lust of the flesh, *in order* to walk in
the Spirit — fighting a battle already lost. What God has said to
you is this, "Walk in the Spirit," in an attitude of total dependence
upon Him, exposing everything to Him, "and you will not fulfill

the lusts of the flesh"—for you will then be enjoying through Him the victory that Christ has already won. To walk in the Spirit is not a *reward*—it is the means! It is to enjoy the Saving Life of Christ!

As you take every step in an attitude of total dependence upon the Lord Jesus Christ who indwells you by His Spirit, He celebrates in you the victory He has already won over sin and death and Satan.

As Moses held his hand high—a picture of the appropriation by faith of God-given victory—Joshua prevailed, and—

. . . discomforted Amalek and his people with the edge of the sword. And the Lord said unto Moses, Write this for a memorial in a book, and rehearse it in the ears of Joshua: for I will utterly put out the remembrance of Amalek from under heaven. And Moses built an altar, and called the name of it Jehovah-nisi [*the Lord my banner*]: For he said, Because the Lord hath sworn that the Lord will have war with Amalek from generation to generation (Exodus 17:13-16).

There will never come a day when God will be at peace with Amalek!

God says of you that in your flesh dwells no good thing, and no flesh will ever glory in His presence— Romans 7:18 and I Corinthians 1:29. Remember what the flesh is—"that spirit that now worketh in the children of disobedience," which first found expression at the fall of Satan when he said in his heart,

I will ascend into heaven, I will exalt my throne above the stars of God: I will sit also upon the mount of the congregation, in the sides of the north: I will ascend above the heights of the clouds; I will be like the most High (Isaiah 14:13,14).

He wanted to *have* something, to *do* something and *be* something, apart from God, and it is this satanic ambition which the flesh seeks to perpetrate in you. The flesh is all that you become in seeking to *have* and to *do* and to *be*, apart from what Christ is — and God is at war from generation to generation with this satanic principle which makes you what you are, apart from what Christ is.

Is there any good reason why Amalek should represent the flesh? What is the characteristic of Amalek that gives to us a legitimate, scriptural reason for seeking in him the picture of the fallen nature of a fallen man?

We must turn to a significant passage in Genesis 25, the

relevance of which may not at first seem apparent, but we read in verse 29:

> And Jacob boiled pottage: and Esau came from the field, and he was faint: And Esau said to Jacob, Feed me, I pray thee, with that same red pottage; for I am faint: therefore was his name called Edom . . . And Jacob said, Swear to me this day: and he sware unto him: and he sold his birthright unto Jacob. Then Jacob gave Esau bread and pottage of lentiles; and he did eat and drink, and rose up, and went his way: thus Esau despised his birthright.

What was the birthright that Esau despised, and which Jacob was to inherit? The birthright was this — the promise that God had given to Abraham that in his seed all the families of the earth should be blessed, not, as Paul points out in Galatians 3, ". . . seeds, as of many; but as of one, and to thy seed, which is Christ." That is to say, the birthright involved the birth of Christ — the Seed of Abraham in particular, through the seed of Abraham in general, the One who would redeem man from his lost condition, and restore him to his true relationship to God, — making him dependent once more upon the One whose presence is life, and who alone can enable man to behave as man, as God intended man to be.

This was the birthright — that God was prepared in the person of His incarnate Son, to make man man again, and to restore him to his true humanity—and Esau despised the birthright! Esau said in his heart, "Sunday school talk! I don't need this kind of kid's stuff! I have all that it takes to be man, apart from God!" There was perpetuated in him the basic lie perpetrated by Satan in Adam — "You are what you are, by virtue of what you are, and not by virtue of what God is. You can lose God and lose nothing!"

In Esau the spirit of Satan was incarnate. "What do I need of a birthright restoring me to dependence upon God? I am independent, and I am self-sufficient, and I will be what I am, by virtue of what I am!"

Mind you, in a worldly context, some might have described Esau as a man's man. He was a hunter, with hair on his chest; he could go out into the forest and carve his own dinner! Jacob, on the other hand, was what we all might have described as a "sissy." He was his mother's pet! He stayed home and helped her with the cooking! He was tied to her apron strings; and she did not even let him look for a girl friend until he was seventy years of age! That was Jacob! His name meant "twister," or "cheat," and he was as good as his name! He was a liar, and he was crooked. He lied to his aged father and he double-crossed his brother.

Jacob was a sneak, and purely from a human point of view, Esau had no time for his twin brother! He could *have* the birthright! Esau had persuaded himself that religion was the weakling's crutch, — and if ever there was a man who needed a crutch, it was Jacob!

Esau had no time for any birthright that was calculated to leave him anything other than completely self-sufficient and completely independent; and God can do nothing for a man like that.

> The burden of the word of the Lord to Israel by Malachi. I have loved you, saith the Lord. Yet ye say, Wherein hast thou loved us? Was not Esau Jacob's brother? saith the Lord: yet I loved Jacob, and I hated Esau, and laid his mountains and his heritage waste for the dragons of the wilderness. Whereas Edom saith, We are impoverished, but we will return and build the desert places; thus saith the Lord of hosts, They shall build, but I will throw down; and they shall call them, The border of wickedness, and the people against whom the Lord hath indignation for ever (Malachi 1:1-4).

Why did God hate Esau? Because God can do absolutely nothing with a man who will not admit that he needs anything from God. Esau rejected God's means of grace, he repudiated man's need of God's intervention, he *despised his birthright* — and God never forgave him! This is the basic attitude of sin — it makes God irrelevant to the stern business of living, and gives to man a flattering sense of self-importance, an attitude portrayed by William Henley in the words of his poem "Invictus" —

> It matters not how straight the gate,
> How charged with punishment the scroll,
> I am the master of my fate,
> I am the captain of my soul.

God can do nothing for the man eaten up with the spirit of Esau. The sad thing is that even a Christian may be so impressed with himself and with his own ability that even though he gives lip-service to the fact, he may still see no personal relevance in the indwelling presence of Christ. It will smack to him of mysticism; he will consider such teaching to be exaggeratedly subjective, and will pride himself on being a practical man of action — and thus he too may despise his birthright.

But Jacob, the twister — God *could* do something for him! God could do something for Jacob when he could do nothing for Esau, for although men might legitimately despise Jacob, they did not despise him any more than he despised himself! There were times maybe, when in the darkness and desperately lonely, the tears would course down his cheeks, and he would cry out in his heart, "God, if there is any kind of blessing that you can give to a person like me, that can make me different from what I am — that is what I need, and that is what I want!"

God can get in and God can begin with a man when he comes to the place of total despair, when he ceases to be impressed with what he is and jettisons all expectation in himself. God loved Jacob! He did not love him for what he was — He loved him for what He could make of him; and God never loved *you* for what *you* were. He loved you, and He loves you still for what He knows He can make of you.

God did not love Saul of Tarsus for standing by and consenting to the death of Stephen; He did not love Saul of Tarsus because he was on his way to Damascus, breathing out threatenings and slaughter, there to throw into jail men, women, and children who dared to call upon the Name of the Lord Jesus. God did not love him for that; God loved Saul of Tarsus for what he would become — Paul, an apostle of Jesus Christ "by the will of God"!

God does not love you for what the flesh makes of your human personality, but He does love you for what Christ can make of your human personality — but God can only begin when you admit your need of Christ. Esau never admitted his need!

The vision of Obadiah. Thus saith the Lord God concerning Edom; We have heard a rumour from the Lord, and an ambassador is sent among the heathen, Arise ye, and let us rise up against her in battle. Behold, I have made thee small among the heathen: thou art greatly despised. The pride of thine heart hath deceived thee, thou that dwellest in the clefts of the rock, whose habitation is high; that saith in his heart, Who shall bring me down to the ground? Though thou exalt thyself as the eagle, and though thou set thy nest among the stars, thence will I bring thee down, saith the Lord. . . . How are the things of Esau searched out! how are his hidden things sought up! (Obadiah 1-4, 6).

This was the spirit of Esau — "I will set myself like God above the stars! Birthright? Who wants a miserable birthright? I have all that it takes to be man, apart from God — God can keep His birthright!" So God kept it, and gave it to Jacob, whom He loved!

Jacob wanted everything he could get from God, and although it was twenty weary years before he entered into the fullness of that purpose for which he had been called, God could at least *begin* with Jacob. He began first at Bethel, "the house of God," and continued twenty years later at Peniel, "the face of God," where, graduating from the school of despair, Jacob wrestled with a man who touched his thigh, and asked him, "What is your name?" And Jacob whispered hoarsely, "Cheat — sneak — twister — thief — supplanter — that is my name!" And God said, in effect, "Jacob, that is all I have been waiting for; I have been waiting for you to call yourself *by your own name* — and now I will change it! You shall be called Israel — Prince of God!"

Given the opportunity, God can take the most beggarly elements of humanity, and make a prince out of them. Did you ever get down on your knees and tell God what you know yourself to be? Have you ever called yourself *by your own name*? If you have learned to do that, you have learned the secret of blessing — and God will *change your name*!

Know Your Enemy (Amalek continued)

8

Know Your Enemy
(Amalek continued)

By now you are probably saying to yourself, "What has Esau to do with Amalek?" To discover this we need first to turn to Genesis 36. Let me remind you again of the relentless consistency of the Holy Spirit, so that wherever you see Esau or Mount Seir or Edom in the Word of God, you will know that He is referring to sin, as a principle: to that satanic attitude of self-sufficiency and independence which is characteristic of the flesh — the carnal mind "that is not subject to the law of God, neither indeed can be" (Romans 8:7).

"Thus dwelt Esau in mount Seir: Esau is Edom. These are the generations of Esau, the father of the Edomites in Mount Seir. . . . And Timna was concubine to Eliphaz Esau's son; and she bare to Eliphaz Amalek" (Genesis 36: 8, 9, 12).

Amalek was Esau's grandson! And Malachi tells us that God was at war with Esau from generation to generation, and Exodus 17 tells us that God was at war with Amalek from generation to generation. Perpetuated in Amalek was the profanity of Esau, the man who refused the birthright.

It is interesting to note in verse 31 of chapter 36, "And these are the kings that reigned in the land of Edom, before there reigned any king over the children of Israel." There were kings in Edom *before* there was a king in Israel, and this has interesting spiritual significance.

You were born by nature a child of wrath, and the flesh exercised the authority of the "king of Edom" — Satan — in your life, long before the Holy Spirit exercised the authority of the "King of Israel" — the Lord Jesus Christ. Chronologically, in fallen man, the flesh always precedes the Spirit, and this is consistently illustrated in the picture language of the Bible. Cain, "who was of that wicked one" (I John 3:12), was born before "righteous" Abel (Hebrews 11:4). Ishmael, "born after the flesh," preceded Isaac, "born after the Spirit," (Galatians 4:2). Esau, that "profane person" whom God hated (Hebrews 12:16, 17), was born before Jacob, whom God loved. Saul, who "played the fool" (I Samuel 26:21) and whom God rejected (I Samuel 15:26), reigned before David, the neighbor better than he (I Samuel 15:28) whom Saul feared, for God was with him (I Samuel 18:12).

Notice too what is said of the kings that reigned in Edom, from verse 33 onward — "And Bela died, and Jobab . . . reigned in his stead. And Jobab died, and Husham . . . reigned in his stead. And Husham died, and Hadad . . . reigned in his stead. And Hadad died, and Samlah . . . reigned in his stead. And Samlah died . . . And Saul died . . . And Baal-hanan died. . . . And these are the names of the dukes that came of Esau . . . he is Esau the father of the Edomites." He died — and he died — and he died! The characteristic of the kings of Edom was that they died! They *all* died! The kings of Edom reigned *unto death,* as distinct from the One born later to be King of Israel, who reigns *unto life* — the Promised Seed of Esau's rejected birthright, whose kingdom shall have no end!

If by one man's offence death reigned by one; much more they that receive abundance of grace and the gift of righteousness shall reign in life by one, Jesus Christ. That as sin hath reigned unto death, even so might grace reign through righteousness unto eternal life by Jesus Christ our Lord (Romans 5:17, 21).

As I have already emphasized, you were born by nature a child of wrath, "dead in sins" (Ephesians 2:5), "for to be carnally minded is death" (Romans 8:6), and to be carnally minded simply means that by nature, as the fallen seed of the fallen Adam, your human personality is dominated from birth by "the spirit that now worketh in the children of disobedience"

(Ephesians 2:1), the spirit that repudiates man's dependence upon God, whose presence alone is life, and whose absence is death.

On the other hand, ". . . to be spiritually minded is life and peace" (Romans 8:6), for to be spiritually minded is to recognize always that all that makes you true man is Christ Himself — received, honored, and obeyed as King.

For in Him the whole fulness of Deity (the Godhead), continues to dwell in bodily form — giving complete expression of the divine nature. And you are in Him, made full *and* have come to fulness of life — in Christ you too are filled with the Godhead: Father, Son and Holy Spirit, and reach full spiritual stature (Colossians 2:9, 10 *Amplified New Testament*).

It is the devil's business to prevent your translation "from the power of darkness . . . into the kingdom of God's dear Son" and Amalek, imbued with the spirit of Satan, is unrelenting in his opposition to the prosperity of the Israel of God.

Balak, who was king of the Moabites at that time, sent a message to Balam the prophet, saying,

"Behold, there is a people come out from Egypt: behold, they cover the face of the earth, and they abide over against me: Come now therefore I pray thee, curse me this people; for they are too mighty for me"(Numbers 22:5, 6).

So Balak would have Balaam curse Israel, but in the next chapter we read that Balaam —

. . took up his parable, and said, Balak the king of Moab hath brought me from Aram, out of the mountains of the east, saying, Come, curse me Jacob, and come, defy Israel. How shall I curse, whom God hath not cursed? or how shall I defy, whom the Lord hath not defied? . . . And he took up his parable, and said. . . . I shall see him, but not now; I shall behold him, but not nigh: there shall come a Star out of Jacob, and a Sceptre shall rise out of Israel (Numbers 23:7, 8; 24:15, 17).

This was the birthright! Speaking prophetically, Balaam foreshadowed the birth of the Lord Jesus Christ as the promised Seed of Abraham. "Out of Jacob shall come He that shall have dominion" — the message which was to be re-iterated upon the lips of the Angel Gabriel —

Fear not, Mary: for thou hast found favour with God. And, behold, thou shalt conceive in thy womb, and bring forth a son, and shalt call his name JESUS. He shall be great, and shall be called the Son of the Highest: and the Lord God shall give unto him the throne of his father David: And he shall reign over the house of Jacob for ever; and of his kingdom there shall be no end (Luke 1:30-33).

But in Numbers 24, after this prophetic utterance, we read of Balaam the prophet in verse 20 — "And when he looked on Amalek, and he took up his parable, and said, — Amalek was the first of the nations [*that is to say, Amalek was the first of the nations to fight against Israel, the first to stand astride the path of God's redeemed people in their march onward into the land of Canaan*] but his latter end shall be that he perish for ever."

Compromise with the flesh and you make an unholy alliance with that which is, and always will be, at enmity with God, and whose end is to perish forever — and this, God says, is something to remember!

"Remember what Amalek did unto thee by the way, when ye were come forth out of Egypt; how he met thee by the way, and smote the hindmost of thee, even all that were feeble behind thee, when thou wast faint and weary" (Deuteronomy 25:17, 18).

That is when Amalek hits you! It is when you are faint and weary. It is when you are one of the hindmost. When you are dragging your feet. When you are spiritually low, and the sun is hidden and the skies are dark. When you have withdrawn yourself from the conflict, because you feel the pace is too much for you. When you think you are alone — but you are not alone, for Amalek will be there! With a little chuckle and a giggle, in his own slimy way, Amalek will be there! That is his business, and he will be up to no good thing! ". . . and he feared not God" (Deuteronomy 25:18).

Amalek has no time for God. He is hostile to God. He "is not subject to the law of God, neither indeed can be" (Romans 8:7). He is profane! He despises the birthright!

Remember Amalek!

God says that there is something that you do not have the right to remember, because it is something which God forgets. God says, "Their sins and iniquities will I remember no more" (Hebrews 10:17). It is not that God pretends that you have not sinned. He does not ignore your guilt. He says, "I will remember your sins," but in the light of the shed blood of His dear Son, having remembered your sins — every one of them — He says, "I will remember your sins *no more*." He has put them away as far as the east is from the west (Psalm 103:12). He has put them behind His back (Isaiah 38:17). He has placed them in the depths of the sea (Micah 7:19). Though they were as scarlet, they have become as white as snow; red like crimson, they have become as wool (Isaiah 1:18). God says that you do not have the right to remember what He forgets, and God says, "I will remember your sins—I will remember your sins, but I will remember them *no more!*"

I emphasize this in particular, because there are some who would seek to persuade you that true holiness comes only from rummaging into the background of your wicked past, and in remembering the things that God has forgotten. They make merchandise of your souls, and glory in your shame. It is a masterpiece of satanic subtlety when the devil persuades your flesh to take an unholy pride in the public confession of sin as the price of blessing. Victory, sanctification, revival, the fulness of the Spirit—these cannot be purchased at such a price, for the price has already been paid! To add anything is to repudiate the adequacy of the death of Christ.

Sin should and must be confessed to God, and restitution made where the Spirit of God demands it, but "the blood of Jesus Christ (God's) Son cleanseth us from all sin," and "if we confess our sins, he is faithful and just to forgive us our sins, and to cleanse us from all unrighteousness" (I John 1:7, 9).

Satan is the accuser of the brethren (Revelation 12:10), and he "accuses them before God day and night." Do not allow him to rob you of your joy, or your peace, or your assurance, by a form of spiritual blackmail! *Christ* has been made unto you righteousness, and all that *He is* has been made over to you on the basis of what *He did*—"And they overcame him by the blood of the Lamb, and by the word of their testimony" (Revelation 12:11). The price has been paid, both for your redemption and for your sanctification, and when God forgives, God forgets!

If, however, you do not have the right to *remember* what God *forgets*,—you do not have the right to *forget* what God *remembers*,—and God remembers Amalek! Amalek is the dirty well! Amalek is the poisoned root! Amalek is ". . . the mystery of lawlessness — that hidden principle of rebellion against constituted authority" (II Thesalonians 2:7 *Amplified New Testament*) that is already at work in the world — "who opposeth and exalteth himself above all that is called God, or that is worshipped; so that he as God sitteth in the temple of God, showing himself that he is God" (II Thessalonians 2:4). Amalek is that sin principle of satanic origin, which makes you what you are apart from what God is, and what you *do* (which God is willing to forgive and forget) stems from what you *are* — *this* you dare not and you must not forget!

Recognize the sinfulness of what you have *done*, and you will recognize the relevance, and your need, of what *He did*. Remember the sinfulness of what *you are*, and you will remember the relevance, and your need, of what *He is*. God says, "Remember Amalek"!

In the following chapter, we shall discuss together the tragedy of a man who *forgot to remember!*

The Man Who Forgot to Remember

9

The Man Who
Forgot to Remember

IN THE NINTH CHAPTER OF THE FIRST BOOK OF SAMUEL WE ARE introduced to a promising, lovely young man — winsome, humble, courteous, conscientious, of unusually impressive physique, and one who had a solid sense of responsibility, the one who was ultimately to become the first king of Israel; and yet, at the same time, a young man who was to ruin his life and die a bitter, disappointed old man, because he forgot to remember!

> Samuel also said unto Saul, The Lord sent me to anoint thee to be king over his people, over Israel: now therefore hearken thou unto the voice of the words of the Lord. Thus saith the Lord of hosts, I remember that which Amalek did to Israel, how he laid wait for him in the way, when he came up from Egypt (I Samuel 15:1, 2).

We have already seen in a previous chapter that sometimes the severest penalty that God can inflict upon His people who reject what they need is to give them what they want; and this was equally true when Israel clamored for a king — "that we also may be like all the nations; and that our king may judge us, and go out before us, and fight our battles" (I Samuel 8:20).

God Himself was Israel's king, and it was never in the purpose of God that any other should usurp the place of the One to be born of Mary, who should reign over the house of Jacob forever — but the Lord said unto Samuel, "Hearken unto the voice of the people in all that they say unto thee: for they have not rejected thee, but they have rejected me, that I should not reign over them. . . . Now therefore hearken unto their voice: howbeit yet protest solemnly unto them, and shew them the manner of the king that shall reign over them" (I Samuel

8:7, 9). Thus it was that Saul, "a choice young man, and a goodly" (I Samuel 9:2) was anointed to be the first king of Israel.

In commissioning him to the task, however, Samuel solemnly warned Saul that if he was to be the earthly representative of Israel's heavenly King, it behoved him to know the mind of God, and to do the will of God, and to execute the judgments of God, and the very first thing that God had to say to Saul as king of Israel, was this:

"I remember that which Amalek did to Israel, how he laid wait for him in the way, when he came up from Egypt. Now go and smite Amalek, and utterly destroy all that they have, and spare them not; but slay both man and woman, infant and suckling, ox and sheep, camel and ass" (I Samuel 15:2, 3).

God was at war with Amalek from generation to generation. There was no good thing in Amalek! There was absolutely no salvageable content in Amalek! There was nothing in Amalek upon which God would look with favor. That was God's mind, God's will, and God's judgment concerning Amalek.

But Saul forgot to remember!

Though he smote the Amalekites, Saul ". . . took Agag the king of the Amalekites alive" — a king of Edom, whom God had sentenced to death! He "utterly destroyed all the people with the edge of the sword. But Saul and the people spared Agag and the best of the sheep, and of the oxen, and of the fatlings, and the lambs, and all that was good" — they spared all that was good in what God had totally condemned as bad! ". . . and would not utterly destroy them: but everything that was vile and refuse, that they destroyed utterly." Saul presumed to find something good in what God had condemned. This was the sin of Saul.

He kept the *best* of what God hated!

This is the subtle temptation with which you too are confronted, for the devil will come to you again and again and whisper in your ear that you are not as bad as the Bible makes you out to be, that there is always something good in what you are, apart from what Christ is — that there is always something salvageable in human nature, no matter how bad a man may seem to be.

God, it seemed to them, was taking things too far. His judgment upon Amalek seemed to them to be unwarranted, a fanatical exaggeration of the issues; and so, in defiance of God's word, God's mind, God's will, and God's judgment, they tried to discern between good and bad in what God had wholly rejected.

It is comparatively easy to be sorry for what you have done and to recognize the sinfulness of sins committed, but we are by nature loathe to concede the natural depravity of what we are and the total spiritual bankruptcy of man without God. We fall again and again into the error of estimating ourselves without due regard to the ultimate origin of righteousness and the ultimate origin of sinfulness.

Let me remind you again that nothing is good or bad by virtue of what it is.

It is good or bad only by virtue of its origin, and that is why you can be so easily deceived and impressed by the pseudo-righteousness and apparent virtue which stem from the self-life, with its perverted bent for simulating what is good.

The apostle voiced his complaint of the Hebrew Christians in the following language —

> Concerning this we have much to say which is hard to explain, since you have become dull in your [spiritual] hearing *and* sluggish, *even* slothful [in achieving spiritual insight]. For even though by this time you ought to be teaching others, you actually need someone to teach you over again the very first principles of God's Word. You have come to need milk, not solid food. For every one who continues to feed on milk is obviously inexperienced *and* unskilled in the doctrine of righteousness, [that is, of conformity to the divine will in purpose, thought and action], for he is a mere infant — not able to talk yet! (Hebrews 5:11-13 *Amplified New Testament*).

The Hebrew believers had forgotten "first principles"; they were "sluggish in achieving spiritual insight"; they were "unskilled in the doctrine of righteousness." What was the measure of their spiritual immaturity that kept them "on the bottle"? Simply that milk is for babies, and that "strong meat belongeth to them that are of full age, even those who by reason of use have their senses exercised to discern both good and evil" (Hebrews 5:14).

They could of course discern between what was obviously good and what was obviously evil — even the youngest child can do that — but because of their ignorance of the fundamental nature of sin (which is every attitude or activity which has its origin other than in God, no matter how pious its context), they were unable to discern between the *genuinely good,* with its origin in God, and the evil in the "good," which has its origin in Satan.

"And no marvel; for Satan himself is transformed into an angel of light. Therefore it is no great thing if his ministers also be transformed as the ministers of righteousness; whose end shall be according to their works" (II Corinthians 11:14, 15).

In other words, the fact that you are a preacher, the fact that you are a missionary, the fact that you are a Christian worker, the fact that you are a witnessing Christian, does not make *you* spiritual, nor your *activity* righteous — no matter how deep your sense of dedication, or the sacrifice involved.

As far as God is concerned, Christ is the preacher, Christ is the missionary, Christ is the Christian worker, Christ is the witnessing Christian. Only what *He* is, and what *He* does, is righteousness — and what He is and what He does is only released through you by your unrelenting attitude of dependence. This is called faith — and ". . . whatsoever is not of faith is sin" (Romans 14:23).

It is a shock to discover that you can go up into the pulpit with a Bible in your hand, preach a sermon entirely Scriptural in its content, and yet if this be done in anything other than an attitude of total dependence upon Christ, in the very act of preaching you are committing sin.

This is not milk for babies, but meat for the strong, who are "of full age," but "hard to be uttered" (Hebrews 5:11), for we have become accustomed to the elaborate machinery of the church, as an organizational enterprise in which carnal activity on the part of Christians is not only tolerated, but solicited—often in sublime sincerity, and with a false sense of dedication on the part of those involved, who, being ignorant of the "very first principles of God's Word," are "unskilled in the doctrine of righteousness."

The flesh does not take kindly to an exposure of the phoney nature of its righteousness. It will be hurt, offended, indignant and resentful, and will seek to justify itself.

> Then came the word of the Lord unto Samuel, saying, It repenteth me that I have set up Saul to be king: for he is turned back from following me, and hath not performed my commandments. And it grieved Samuel; and he cried unto the Lord all night. . . . And Samuel came to Saul: and Saul said unto him, Blessed be thou of the Lord; I have performed the commandment of the Lord. And Samuel said, What meaneth then this bleating of the sheep in mine ears, and the lowing of the oxen which I hear? And Saul said, They have brought them from the Amalekites: for the people spared the best of the sheep and of the oxen, to sacrifice unto the Lord thy God; and the rest we have utterly destroyed (I Samuel 15:11-15).

The bleating of the sheep and the lowing of the oxen did little to vindicate Saul's claim that he had performed the commandment of the Lord, but symptomatic of the man who "has forgotten to remember," Saul saw no inconsistency in this. Instead, assuming an air of offended innocence, he insisted that he had not only performed the commandment of the Lord, but had done so with *superior judgment* — the fact that the people had spared the best of the sheep, and the best of the oxen, and the best of the lambs, was the only reasonable, sensible, logical, economical thing to do — but of course, only to sacrifice them to the Lord!

Saul said in so many words, "Don't get me wrong! Don't do us the injustice of misjudging our motives! The good that we have found in Amalek, we have kept to dedicate to God." It is a stroke of satanic genius, and one of his most ancient devices, to persuade you piously to dedicate to God all that you presume to find good in the flesh which God has condemned.

This is the curse of Christendom! This is what paralyzes the activity of the Church of Jesus Christ on earth today! In defiance of God's Word, God's mind, God's will, and God's judgment, men everywhere are prepared to dedicate to God what God condemns — the energy of the flesh!

All too characteristic of church-life today is the bleating of the sheep in the pew, and the lowing of the oxen in the pulpit!

No matter how much it may cost you, no matter how much sacrifice it may involve, and no matter how great your enthusiasm or your sincerity, the best that you can salvage from Amalek will be an offering unseasoned with salt, and will be repudiated by God as Saul himself was repudiated.

"Then Samuel said unto Saul, Stay, and I will tell thee what the Lord hath said to me this night. . . Behold, to obey is better than sacrifice, and to hearken than the fat of rams. For rebellion is as the sin of witchcraft, and stubbornness is as iniquity and idolatry. Because thou has rejected the word of the Lord, he hath also rejected thee from being king" (I Samuel 15:16, 22, 23).

God rejected Saul because he forgot to remember!

Instead of the winsome, humble, courteous, thoughtful young man, to whom we were first introduced in I Samuel 9, he became a bitter, murderous, wicked old man, who could only look back upon a wasted life and say, "I have sinned. . . . Behold, I have played the fool, and have erred exceedingly" (I Samuel 26:21). He presumed to find good in what God had condemned, and God rejected him.

In his anguish of soul after the death of Samuel, he solicited the aid of a woman with a familiar spirit, and when Samuel appeared, Saul answered him,

> I am sore distressed; for the Philistines make war against me, and God is departed from me, and answereth me no more, neither by prophets, nor by dreams: therefore I have called thee, that thou mayest make known unto me what I shall do. Then said Samuel, Wherefore then dost thou ask of me, seeing the Lord is departed from thee, and is become thine enemy? Because thou obeyedst not the voice of the Lord, nor executedst his fierce wrath upon Amalek, therefore hath the Lord done this thing unto thee this day (I Samuel 28:15, 16, 18).

God had said, "Remember Amalek," and Saul forgot to remember!

Saul had repudiated God's verdict on Amalek; now he was to learn the hard and bitter way that God's verdict was right. Though you may show mercy to Amalek, Amalek will never show mercy to you!

This, of course, is the key to the book of Esther; for Haman, the "enemy of the Jews" who hatched the murderous plot for their total annihilation, was an Agagite — a descendant

of Agag, king of the Amalekites, whose life Saul spared
(Esther 3:1).

Saul attempted to commit suicide, but he did not succeed. Just how he died is described in the first chapter of II
Samuel:

"A man came out of the camp from Saul with his clothes
rent. . . . And David said unto him, From whence comest
thou? . . . How went the matter? . . . And he answered,
That the people are fled from the battle, and many of the
people also are fallen and dead; and Saul and Jonathan his
son are dead also" (II Samuel 1:2-4).

David inquired of this young man how he could be so
sure of his facts, and the young man replied,

"As I happened by chance upon mount Gilboa, behold,
Saul leaned upon his spear; and, lo, the chariots and horse-
men followed hard after him. And when he looked behind
him, he saw me, and called unto me. And I answered,
Here am I. And he said unto me, Who art thou? And I
answered him, *I am an Amalekite*" (6-8).

Oh yes, whenever you are down, there will always be an Amalekite around! In your hour of greatest temptation and despair,
"faint and weary," you will always hear his sadistic whisper in
your ear, "I am an Amalekite; I am always here when you *need*
me! It is my job to hit a man when he is down — and it is my
job to destroy him! I am an Amalekite! That is my business!"

Continuing his story to David, the Amalekite said, "He
said unto me again, Stand, I pray thee, upon me, and slay me.
. . . So I stood upon him, and slew him . . . and I took the crown
that was upon his head. . . ." He slew him, *and he took
his crown!*

You compromise with Amalek at your peril! In your
flesh dwells *no good thing*. Spare it if you will, but it will never
spare you! Presume to find something good in it, when God has
wholly condemned it, and the day will come when it will destroy
you and rob you of your crown! God says that no flesh will
ever glory in His presence. It can only make your body the
devil's plaything, so that he can be incarnate in all you say and
do, robbing Christ of His rightful sovereignty in your humanity,

whose life alone constitutes the true and only source of genuine righteousness.

Are you still offering to God the *best* of what God has *condemned?*

With the Promised Land only eleven days journey away, "then came Amalek," and for forty years they wandered in the wilderness, grieving God in self-imposed poverty, robbed of all that for which they had been redeemed!

Do not be deceived by Amalek! Resist him with the rod of God held high, appropriating the victory already won. Carve your way through his ranks, for this is your victory, even your faith! Go *on* and go *in*, thanking the Lord Jesus for his LIFE, as you have learned to thank Him for His DEATH — for what He IS, as you have learned to thank Him for what He DID! Christ is your Victory!

"Behold, I come quickly: hold that fast which thou hast, *that no man take thy crown!*" (Revelation 3:11).

The Man Who Died Too Young

10

The Man Who
Died Too Young

THE BOOK OF DEUTERONOMY IS IN SOME SENSES ONE OF THE
saddest books in the Bible, for it is the last will and testament of
a disappointed man. It is the record of all that Moses had to say
to the children of Israel, on the first day of the eleventh month
of the fortieth year of their wanderings in the Wilderness.

"These be the words which Moses spake unto all Israel on
this side Jordan in the wilderness, in the plain over against
the Red Sea. . . ." (Deuteronomy 1:1).

On the wrong side of Jordan, and only just on the right
side of the Red Sea! And this forty years after Moses had led his
people out of Egypt.

Of those who died in the wilderness, it is written, "So
we see that they could not enter in because of unbelief"
(Hebrews 3:19), and it is a sobering thought to realize that
Moses too died in the wilderness, numbered among the "unbelieving believers" — those who had faith enough to get out, but
who did not have faith enough to get in.

Moses was a spiritual giant. "And there arose not a
prophet since in Israel like unto Moses, whom the Lord knew
face to face" (Deuteronomy 34:10). He was unmatched for
his sheer, moral integrity; unmatched in his selfless sense of
duty, in his tireless concern for the people whom he served, in
his nobility of character, and in his humble dedication to God.
It would seem that if ever a man deserved to get into Canaan
it was Moses — but he died in the wilderness!

"And Moses was an hundred and twenty years old when
he died: his eye was not dim, nor his natural force abated"
(Deuteronomy 34:7).

117

There was no physical cause of death. Moses died *too young,* and he was buried *in the wrong place!*

"So Moses the servant of the Lord died there in the land of Moab, according to the word of the Lord. And he buried him in a valley in the land of Moab, over against Bethpeor: but no man knoweth of his sepulchre unto this day" (Deuteronomy 34:5 and 6).

It seems that the lesson that God would have us learn is of such supreme importance and so universal in its application that He purposely chose one of the choicest of His servants, lest any should consider themselves to be excused. God loved Moses, and I cannot help but be convinced that he will be numbered among the aristocracy of heaven in the vast company of the redeemed — yet the very severity with which God dealt with him serves only to emphasize the importance that God attaches to the principle he violated.

Add to his nobility of character the fact that Moses was a great leader, a great preacher, a great administrator, a man of immense mental stature, and almost everything else that you or I might seek to emulate, embodying all our highest and holiest ambitions — and you have a man whom one cannot help but admire and respect. And yet in spite of all this, he died a disappointed man! He never entered the land! He was sick of his ministry, sick of the people to whom he ministered, and they were equally sick of him!

You will remember how at the outset of the journey, God had commanded Moses to smite the rock in Horeb, that water might flow for the children of Israel in the thirsty Wilderness of Sin, on the east of the Gulf of Suez. Then some 38 years later, the children of Israel came to the desert of Zin, west of the south end of the Salt Sea, and there was no water for the congregation. In 38 years, all that Moses had succeeded in doing was to lead the people from one geographical location in the desert to another, from the desert of Sin to the desert of Zin. He had changed an S into a Z, and both are made out of a crooked "I"!

No matter how gifted you may be, or how great your enthusiasm; no matter what kind of an orator, or how dynamic your personality; no matter what your social standing; no matter how popular or famous you may become, the best that you can ever do in the wilderness, with your own life or with the lives of any others to whom you may minister, is to twist the crooked "I" into some new, crooked shape!

Some have imagined that the cure for their spiritual disability is a change of geographical location, a call to a new pastorate, or exchange of field or occupation, but if you are living in the wilderness, you will be as useless in one part of the desert as you are in another!

> And the people chode with Moses, and spake, saying, Would God that we had died when our brethren died before the Lord! And why have ye brought up the congregation of the Lord into this wilderness, that we and our cattle should die there? Wherefore have ye made us to come up out of Egypt, to bring us into this evil place? it is no place of seed, or of figs, or of vines, or of pomegranates; neither is there any water to drink (Numbers 20:3-5).

Having sat under Moses' preaching for nearly forty years, all that they could say of the place to which he had brought them was that it was an evil place — "no place of seed, or of figs, or of vines, or of pomegranates" — as dry and as thirsty as the place where the journey began. Is that the normal Christian life? Is that really all you may expect?

As a pastor or a missionary or a Sunday school teacher, would you like those to whom you have ministered to tell you after 38 years that the place to which you have brought them is an evil place, that it has fallen completely short of anything that you gave them to believe?

The children of Israel knew all about Canaan in their heads, for Moses had preached about it until they were tired of the sound of it — the only thing he did *not* do was to take them there! It is a weary business preaching Canaan in the wilderness! It is language without life, sentiment without substance.

"And the Lord spake unto Moses, saying: Take the rod and gather thou the assembly together, thou and Aaron thy brother, and speak ye unto the rock before their eyes" (7-8).

What was Moses told to do the first time in Horeb in the Wilderness of Sin? He was told to smite the rock — a picture of Jesus Christ and Him crucified.

What was he told to do now?

He was told to *speak* to the rock — a picture of the Lord Jesus Christ risen from the dead, and ascended to the Father, who "after He had offered one sacrifice for sins for ever, sat down on the right hand of God" (Hebrews 10:12), whose body will never again be broken, and whose blood will never again be shed.

"Speak ye unto the rock . . . and it shall give forth his water, and thou shalt bring forth to them water out of the rock."

God's instructions were explicit. The rock was not again to be smitten, for ". . . by one offering He hath perfected for ever them that are sanctified" (Hebrews 10:14). We may not now seek the living among the dead, for He is risen and glorified! God said, "Speak ye unto the rock"!

Moses, however, addressed his congregation, "Hear now, ye rebels. . . ." Is that how you would like to speak to *your* congregation, after nearly forty years of ministry? "Hear now, ye rebels; must *we* fetch you water out of this rock?"

No, God did not tell Moses to fetch water out of the rock. God told Moses to *speak* to the rock, and the rock would *give* all the water that they needed. "For," said the Lord Jesus Christ, "He that believeth on me, out of his innermost being shall flow rivers of living water; but this spake he of the Spirit, whom they that believe on him should receive, for the Holy Ghost was not yet given, because that Jesus was not yet glorified" (John 7:38, 39).

Reconciled to God by His death — the smitten rock — you are to be saved by His life — the living Rock.

The Christian life is the life that the Lord Jesus Christ lived nineteen hundred years ago, *lived now by Him in you!* All things that pertain to life and godliness have been given to you in Him, as a partaker of the divine nature (II Peter 1:3, 4).

"And Moses lifted up his hand and with his rod he smote the rock twice . . ." (Numbers 20:11) — the rock that might only be smitten once! He left Christ on the cross! In the language of the illustration, he was a man with only half a message. He declared the crucified Christ, but not the risen Lord! And a man with only half a message does only half a job! He got them out, but he did not get them in!

Moses preached his people to tears of repentance again

and again — but he never got them in! He wooed and he threatened them, rebuked and encouraged them, and with tireless integrity, he stood in the gap and interceded for them; but they returned again and again to their backsliding. He never got them in!

This should be a solemn warning to each one of us, for we too, if we preach only half a message, will do only half a job. We too will be loaded with a bunch of spiritual babies, and with Moses, it will be our unhappy lot to fill their bottles and push them around in the wilderness! We may succeed in getting them out, but we shall never succeed in getting them in!

"And the Lord spake unto Moses and Aaron, Because ye believed me not, to sanctify me in the eyes of the children of Israel, therefore ye shall not bring this congregation into the land which I have given them" (Numbers 20:12).

"Because ye believed me not" — an "unbelieving believer." This was the sin of Moses, a man who died too young and who was buried in the wrong place.

It is almost disconcerting to witness the severity of God's judgment upon this mighty warrior; but he broke the type, he violated the first principle of victorious Christian living — CHRIST IN YOU, the hope of glory! He never got beyond Jesus Christ and Him crucified. In the language of the Old Testament, his Gospel was never more than "Come to Jesus, and have your sins forgiven." It was a message of "heaven some day, but the wilderness now!" He left Christ on the cross! He knew nothing of the Saving Life of Christ.

It is our solemn responsibility, not only to present the Lord Jesus Christ as the One Who died historically to redeem sinners through His atoning sacrifice, but as a contemporary experience NOW — as the living Rock, the source of that "pure river of water of life, clear as crystal, proceeding out of the throne of God and of the Lamb" (Revelation 22:1).

I am deeply grateful to those who introduced me to the Lord Jesus Christ as my Redeemer, but the one thing that they did not make adequately clear to me (because in all probability it was inadequately clear to them) was that the Christ who died *for* me, rose again to live *in* me. So, knowing Christ experientially only as the Way, it took seven weary years to come to know Him as my Life.

At the age of nineteen, training at London University to become a doctor in order to serve as a missionary in Africa, I knew that my life as a Christian was ineffective. I did not know of one single soul whom it had been my privilege to lead to Christ. I engaged in more than my share of Christian activity, and with genuine enthusiasm, but I knew that if I ever went as a missionary to Africa, I would be just as useless there.

It was out of a deep sense of need, as I despaired of my Christian life, that I made the startling discovery that for seven years I had missed the whole point of my salvation, that Christ had not died just to save me from hell and one day get me to heaven, but that I might become available to Him — for Him to live His life through me.

For all those years I had known only the shadow of the smitten Rock in Horeb, but now at last in the bright light of day, I stepped out by faith to speak to the living Rock, and life for me as a Christian was transformed; the rivers of living water began to flow.

God gave me nothing new. I had simply discovered what I already had, Christ in all His fullness *in me*, "the hope of glory."

The sad thing is that it is all too possible to become accustomed to living in the wilderness, especially when we are surrounded by wilderness Christians, and it is almost with dismay that we read that Moses, who once told Joshua to go out and fight with Amalek, ". . . sent messengers from Kadesh unto the king of Edom, Thus saith thy brother Israel . . ." (Numbers 20:14).

It seems that after 38 years Moses had come to terms with Amalek. But this is axiomatic, for it is the living, risen Lord who must take the place of that old Adamic nature; but if you know Him only as the smitten Rock, a crucified Redeemer, no matter how grateful you may be to Him, and no matter how strong the urge to follow in His ways, you will, like the foolish Galatians, ". . . having begun in the Spirit," try to be "made perfect by the flesh." You will have to come to terms with

Amalek, and call him your brother, for you will know of nothing
that can take his place.

However, although Moses' attitude toward Amalek had
changed, the attitude of Amalek toward Moses had not changed.
"Edom said unto him, Thou shalt not pass by me, lest I come
out against thee with the sword." In other words, said Amalek,
— "thirty-eight years ago I withstood you to your face, and I
have not changed *my* mind — I withstand you still! Thou shalt
not pass!" It was his business to keep God's people out of
Canaan. "Thus Edom [*Esau, Amalek,*] refused to give Israel
passage through his border; wherefore Israel turned away from
him" (Numbers 20:21). Where was the rod held high? Where
was their God-given victory? God had commanded them to go
north — and they turned south! God said, "Go on" — and they
went back!

> . . . We compassed mount Seir many days. And the Lord spake unto
> me, saying, Ye have compassed this mountain long enough: turn you
> northward. And command thou the people, saying, Ye are to pass
> through the coast of your brethren the children of Esau, which dwell in
> Seir; and they shall be afraid of you: take ye good heed unto yourselves
> therefore: Meddle not with them; for I will not give you of their land,
> no, not so much as a foot breadth; because I have given mount Seir unto
> Esau for a possession (Deuteronomy 2:1-5).

There was to be no possession for Israel in the land of
Edom, and they were not to meddle with the children of Esau.
They were to go on northward, onward into the land which God
had given them, and their enemies would be afraid of them. But
alas, it was the children of Israel who were afraid, and they
"journeyed from Kadesh, and came unto mount Hor. . . . And
they journeyed from mount Hor by the way of the Red Sea, to
compass the land of Edom: and the soul of the people was much
discouraged because of the way." (Numbers 20:22; 21:4).

It was at this point that they crossed the brook Zered
in the direction of Moab and Ammon, *on the wrong side* of
Jordan, which now lay between them and the land of promise,
and, said Moses, ". . . The space in which we came from Kadesh-
Barnea [*from where the twelve spies were sent into Canaan*],
until we were come over the brook Zered, was thirty and eight
years" — thwarted from start to finish by Amalek, who refused
to give Israel passage through his borders.

Just suppose that, with the rod held high, Israel had

obeyed God's word in Kadesh-Barnea, separated as it was from the Land of Promise only by a small piece of the land of Edom! Just suppose that then they had listened to the "two," instead of to the "ten," and had gone on and gone in — there would have been no Jordan to cross!

There was no Jordan between Kadesh-Barnea and Canaan. Jordan lay to the east, and the crossing of the Jordan only became a necessity in the experience of Israel because instead of going *through,* they went *round* the land of Edom.

In forty years of compromise, of unbelief and disobedience, the children of Israel had forgotten what God had tried to teach them in their miraculous deliverance from Egypt, bringing them by faith through the place of death, the Red Sea, and raising them again into newness of life, so that this lesson had to be learned all over again at Jordan.

How true this is to Christian experience. If only we could grasp at the outset the deeper significance of the cross, that Christ not only died for us, but that we died with Him, that He rose again to live in the power of His Holy Spirit within us, and that we are to be partakers of Christ now, as the children of Israel should have been partakers of the land then! (Hebrews 3:14). Then we could get out and get out quickly, and we could get in and get in quickly, and begin to explore the land all at once, and we would never have to learn the true significance of the cross a second time.

Unfortunately, because of the stubborn nature of the human heart, because of the deep roots of the flesh within the area of our human personality, it often takes months and years, and sometimes a lifetime before a Christian is brought to the place where he can relearn at Jordan what he should have learned at the Red Sea.

Sometimes people talk about a second blessing, and I know what they mean, and I will not argue with them — but it is not really a second blessing. It is simply a rediscovery of the first blessing!

When you come to know Jesus Christ in the power of His resurrection, you receive absolutely nothing new from God; you simply discover and begin to enjoy experientially what you received from God the day that you were redeemed; the tragedy is that you can live for ten, twenty, or fifty years or more, having all that God can give you in Jesus Christ, and yet living in self-imposed poverty — out, but not in — and that is why Jordan so often, unfortunately, is necessary.

It is the place where, under Joshua, God had to re-teach the children of Israel what, under Moses, the children of Israel had forgotten.

Now after the death of Moses the servant of the Lord it came to pass, that the Lord spake unto Joshua the son of Nun, Moses' minister, saying, Moses my servant is dead; now therefore arise, go over this Jordan, thou, and all this people, unto the land which I do give to them, even to the children of Israel (Joshua 1:1, 2).

The use of the word "therefore" implies the conclusion of an argument. It speaks of cause and effect, and God said to Joshua, "Moses my servant is dead; go, therefore . . ." In other words, "*Because* Moses my servant is dead — *therefore* go!"

Can it really be true that the final obstacle to the onward march of God's people into their inheritance, was Moses himself? That the man who *built* the Church in the Wilderness was the man who *buried* it in the wilderness? That there could be no spiritual change of climate until he was out of the way? This, it seems, is the inescapable conclusion to which we are forced.

You may think that I am being too rough on Moses, that it is not fair to blame him. You may argue in his defence that the children of Israel did not *want* to get in. Then I must ask you a simple question. Did they want to get out?

And when Pharaoh drew nigh, the children of Israel lifted up their eyes, and, behold, the Egyptians marched after them; and they were sore afraid: and the children of Israel cried out unto the Lord. And they said unto Moses, Because there were no graves in Egypt, hast thou taken us away to die in the wilderness? Wherefore hast thou dealt thus with us, to carry us forth out of Egypt? Is not this the word that we did tell thee in Egypt, saying, Let us alone, that we may serve the Egyptians? For it had been better for us to serve the Egyptians, than that we should die in the wilderness (Exodus 14:10-12).

No, the record is clear, — they did *not* want to get out. It was in spite of their protests that Moses led them out of Egypt. Had they had their way, they would have stayed there. "Let us alone," they said, "that we may serve the Egyptians," but some-how Moses knew how to teach them the kind of faith that gets out, though he did not know how to teach them the kind of faith that gets in.

And Moses said unto the people, Fear ye not, stand still, and see the salvation of the Lord, which He will shew to you today: for the Egyptians whom ye have seen today, ye shall see them again no more for ever. The Lord shall fight for you, and ye shall hold your peace. . . . And the people feared the Lord, and believed the Lord, and His servant Moses (Exodus 14:13, 14, 31).

Why is it that a man who could lead an unwilling people out was unable to lead an unwilling people in? This is the problem with which so many are confronted, who enjoy a measure of success in their evangelistic activity, but whose converts are of such poor spiritual caliber; who find it comparatively easy to precipitate the crisis of decision, but are baffled by the ensuing lack of spiritual substance in those who have made profession of faith.

It is to the solution of this problem that this book is dedicated.

Forgive me if I have seemed to be unduly severe in my treatment of Moses. Believe me, I have the deepest admiration for this mighty man of God, and it is evidence of the high esteem in which God held him that he was numbered among those who stood with the Lord Jesus upon the Mount of Transfiguration, when at last he was allowed into the land.

I believe that God deliberately chose this noble man, through whom to teach us this essential lesson, that all of us might be without excuse.

God would have us know without any shadow of ambiguity that no degree of human excellence can ever be a substitute for His dear Son. Moses did his best! His very, very best — but this was the mistake that Moses made! For God was waiting to do God's best, to give what only can be given, from the risen, living Rock.

The Rock that God smites once, let no man smite again! — or die too young! When God says speak, then speak! God will do the rest!

". . . This is the work of God that ye believe on him whom he hath sent" (John 6:29).

"O come, let us sing unto the Lord: let us make a joyful noise to the rock of our salvation. Let us come before His presence with thanksgiving, and make a joyful noise unto Him with psalms. For the Lord is a great God, and a great King above all gods" (Psalm 95:1-3).

The Man With the Sword in His Hand

11

The Man With the Sword
in His Hand

THE FUNDAMENTAL CHARACTERISTIC OF TRUTH IS ITS CON-
sistency.

In the face of every known and unknown fact, truth
must remain inviolably consistent. It is final and absolute.
Circumstance cannot change truth. If circumstance compels
you to re-think previous conclusions, and if honesty, in the light
of new information, compels you to change your convictions,
it does not mean that the truth has changed — it simply means
that you never knew the truth, and that circumstance or addi-
tional information are compelling you to recognize the fact.

In His prayer to the Father for those who believe on
Him, the Lord Jesus said, "Sanctify them through thy truth: thy
word is truth" (John 17:17). Truth is not academic. It is the
ultimate principle of life, and sanctification is this principle in
action — truth in action!

This was the perfection of the Manhood of the Lord
Jesus. He was The Truth — incarnate, and its final exegesis.

Truth obeyed in the human heart identifies the believer
instantly with Jesus Christ. He said, "Everyone that is of the
truth heareth my voice" (John 18:37), and again, "If ye continue in my word, then are ye my disciples indeed; and ye shall
know the truth, and the truth shall make you free" (John
8:31, 32).

Man's spiritual emancipation takes place when he returns to truth — that is to say, when he returns to basic first
principles, and these have never changed.

We may miss them, we may depart from them, we may

misinterpret them, but God's principles do not change. God does not need new methods, He does not need a new technique. He uses any means, any method, any technique. That is immaterial. It is purely secondary. All that is accomplished to God's ultimate satisfaction and of eternal worth, no matter what the means, is always the consequence of a return to first principles.

That is why, all down the history of the Church, every spiritual awakening and every mighty movement of God has been the consequence of a return to the basic teachings of the Bible, and inevitably, in reverse, such a genuine spiritual awakening has always produced Bible believing Christians.

This is one of the main lessons that we learn from the book of Joshua.

"Every place that the sole of your foot shall tread upon, that have I given unto you, as I said unto Moses" (Joshua 1:3).

Forty years had passed since God had brought the children of Israel out of Egypt, and Moses was dead; but God had not changed His mind. "Hath he said, and shall he not do it? or hath he spoken, and shall he not make it good?" (Numbers 23:19). The principle that God employed in bringing them out was the principle that God intended to employ in bringing them in, and God was simply waiting for the man who would return to this principle. "As I was with Moses [in bringing the children of Israel out of Egypt] so I will be with thee [in bringing them into Canaan]. . . . Have not I commanded thee?" — that is why! "Be strong and of a good courage; be not afraid, neither be thou dismayed; for the Lord thy God is with thee whithersoever thou goest" — that is how! That is the why and the how of all spiritual activity, and this is all you need to know.

Why? God told me to.

How? The God who told me to is with me.

This is the principle that the Lord Jesus Himself demonstrated. "For I do always those things which please Him." In other words, in all that He did at any given moment, the Lord Jesus could say, "He told me to." And because of this fact, He could go on to say, "And He that sent me is with me: the Father hath not left me alone." In other words, "The One who told me to is with me" (John 8:29).

"Then Joshua commanded the officers of the people, saying, Pass through the host, and command the people, saying, Prepare you victuals; for within three days ye shall pass over this Jordan, to go in to possess the land, which the Lord your God giveth you to possess it" (Joshua 1:10, 11).

Had he been alive to hear this message from Joshua to the people, a lesser man than Moses might well have said, with all the bitterness of sour grapes, "Is this swollen-headed young upstart going to try to do in three days what I could not do in forty years?" And the answer, of course, would have been quite simple. Joshua was going to *try* to do nothing — he had simply returned to first principles!

Moses was the man who *tried,* and he gave them the law without the land! Joshua was the man who *trusted,* and he gave them the land in which to practice the law!

And on the third day, early in the morning, they were in!

Does this remind you of anything? What happened on the third day early in the morning? Jesus Christ rose again from the dead! And this is the land — to know Him in the power of His resurrection.

We were buried therefore with Him by the baptism into death, so that just as Christ was raised from the dead by the glorious [power] of the Father, so we too might habitually live *and* behave in newness of life. For if we have become one with Him by sharing a death like His, we shall also be [one with Him in sharing] His resurrection [by a new life lived for God] (Romans 6:4, 5 *Amplified New Testament*). If then you have been raised with Christ [to a new life, thus sharing His resurrection from the dead], aim at *and* seek the [rich, eternal treasures] that are above, where Christ is, seated at the right hand of God. For [as far as this world is concerned] you have died, and your [new, real] life is hid with Christ in God (Colossians 3:1, 3 *Amplified New Testament*).

[For my determined purpose is] that I may know Him. . . . And that I may in that same way come to know the power outflowing from His resurrection [which it exerts over believers] . . . That if possible I may attain to the [spiritual and moral] resurrection [that lifts me] out from among the dead [even while in the body] (Philippians 3:10, 11 *Amplified New Testament*).

Yes, as we have seen again and again, the land of Canaan is nothing less than the believer's enjoyment, on earth, of the resurrection life of Jesus Christ.

Remembering that of the twelve spies sent by Moses, ten were duds who served only "to discourage the heart of the people" (Deuteronomy 1:28), Joshua streamlined his battle plans and sent only two men to spy secretly, saying, "Go view the land, even Jericho" (Joshua 2:1).

Information reached the ears of the king of Jericho, whose Intelligence Service appears to have been commendably efficient, and but for the timely action of the harlot Rahab, the spies might have come to an untimely end. She hid them on the roof beneath the stalks of the flax, and sent their pursuers on a false trail.

It was from this woman the spies made their amazing discovery —

> And she said unto the men, I know that the Lord hath given you the land, and that your terror is fallen upon us, and that all the inhabitants of the land faint because of you. For we have heard how the Lord dried up the water of the Red Sea for you, when ye came out of Egypt; and what ye did unto the two kings of the Amorites, that were on the other side Jordan, Sihon and Og, whom ye utterly destroyed. And as soon as we had heard these things, our hearts did melt, neither did there remain any more courage in any man, because of you: for the Lord your God, he is God in heaven above, and in earth beneath (Joshua 2:9-11).

The spies made the startling discovery that already for forty years the inhabitants of Canaan had been a defeated foe! They had conceded victory to Israel from the day that they had heard how the Lord dried up the water of the Red Sea for them, when they came out of Egypt. Their hearts had melted and there was no more courage in any of them. They had become convinced that the God of Israel was God in heaven above, and in earth beneath — that He was as competent to get His people in as He was competent to get His people out. The only thing that had amazed them was that Israel had taken so long to *take* what God had given!

The spies discovered that for forty years in the wilderness, Israel had been fighting a battle already lost, instead of enjoying in Canaan a victory already won!

This is the discovery that you too will make when by faith you obey first principles, the discovery that you have been defrauding yourself, maybe for ten, twenty, thirty, forty, or fifty years, of a victory that Christ won over nineteen hundred years ago, when He rose again from the dead that He might live His life in you.

So the two spies hurried back to Joshua to tell him the exciting news —

"Truly the Lord hath delivered into our hands all the land; for even all the inhabitants of the country do faint because of us. . . . And the Lord said unto Joshua, This day will I begin to magnify thee in the sight of all Israel, that they may know that, as I was with Moses, so I will be with thee" (Joshua 2:24; 3:7).

So Joshua gathered all the people to him. He wanted them to know that a new chapter was being opened in the history of Israel, that life for them could never be the same again.

His language was the language of victory, and his faith became infectious. He said,

"Hereby ye shall know that the living God is among you, and that he will without fail drive out from before you the Canaanites. . . . Behold, the ark of the covenant of the Lord of all the earth passeth over before you into Jordan" (Joshua 3:10, 11).

In so many words, Joshua said, "You have been living for forty years in the wilderness as though your God were dead, but you are going to live from now on knowing that your God is alive."

Ignoring what they say, and what they sing, and what they pray, countless Christians *live* as though God were dead — and the Church of Jesus Christ needs above everything else to re-discover the fact that God is alive, and to act as though He were!

Suppose that God were to die tonight! Would it really make any difference to the way you live your Christian life tomorrow? For all you *really* count upon Him as you go about your daily business, or even do your Christian work, would you notice any difference? Would it make the slightest difference next Sunday in the services in your place of worship, if God were to die tonight? Or would it be business as usual? Would anybody know if nobody told them? Or would the whole machine grind on, with the people in the pew, the parson in the pulpit, and the special offering for the building fund! Nobody ever told them that God was dead!

If we dare to face the hard, cold-blooded truth, we would have to admit today that there is so little in the life of our churches, so little in the activity of so many of our missionary societies and Christian organizations that cannot be explained in terms of man's ability and promotional activity, that few would cease to function if God were dead.

We see the evidence of this all around us, in so many enterprises which years ago came into being under the inspiration of Spirit-filled men of God, but which organizationally have slowly outgrown their spiritual content, until nothing of spiritual life remains, and God is no longer consulted in their counsels — but they do not cease to function! They continue to exist, but they do not live. Of these, as of the church in Sardis, God would say, "I know your record *and* what you are doing; you are supposed to be alive, but [in reality] you are dead" (Revelation 3:1 *Amplified New Testament*).

This, however, under Joshua was no longer to be the experience of the children of Israel. They were to know and to enjoy the fact that the living God was among them.

> When ye see the ark of the covenant of the Lord your God, and the priests the Levites bearing it, then ye shall remove from your place, and go after it. Yet there shall be a space between you and it, about two thousand cubits by measure: come not near unto it, that ye may know the way by which ye must go: for ye have not passed this way heretofore (Joshua 3:3, 4).

Without enlarging upon the fact, we should note that the ark represented God's covenant with His people, and what was in it represented the spiritual content of their faith, and God's purpose for their lives. And the ark was to go before them, with a space between it and them.

What a valuable lesson there is for us to learn in this. They were to keep well back from the ark, that they might know the way, and follow it wherever it went. Had they surrounded the ark, nobody would have known the way. There would have been nothing but confusion, with about fifty sub-committees all deliberating the issue!

They were to give God room to maneuver in time and space; they were not to crowd in on the situation, but to keep well back. The Bible records for us so many tragic blunders committed by good, earnest, sincere, well-meaning men in a hurry, who acted precipitately under the pressure of circumstance.

Learn to give God room to maneuver. Learn to be still and to know that He is God. You do not have the right to panic! If you are solidly convinced that God is the arbiter of your affairs, you will never be anxious. "Commit thy way unto the Lord, trust also in Him, and he will bring to pass (act). . . . Rest in the Lord, and wait patiently for Him" (Psalm 37:5, 7).

God knows the way! Remember what God said to Joshua, "Every place that the sole of your foot shall tread upon, that have I given unto you." It was to be one step at a time. "There shall not any man be able to stand before thee all the days of thy life." It was to be one day at a time. One step at a time and one day at a time. This is the daily walk of the man of God. Hurry at your own peril, "for ye have not passed this way heretofore."

This could hardly have been said of the children of Israel in their wanderings in the wilderness, for they had traveled round and round in circles. There was hardly a grain of sand they did not know by name, nor a cactus bush upon which they had not sat! But this was to be a new experience. It was to be the daily exploration of the *land*, with new discoveries to be made and new areas to be possessed with every step they took.

Some wilderness Christians get very angry when you tell them about the indwelling life of the risen Lord Jesus Christ in all His sovereignty, and they are most indignant when you suggest that they have never been this way before.

"Do you mean to tell me," they will say, "that after forty years I still don't know how to live the Christian life?" — and they will shoot off all hot round the collar, to make another accelerated circuit round the course, and try to make up in speed what they lack in direction! If you insist on going round in circles, you will always get back to where you started, and the faster you go the quicker you will get there!

". . . And the people passed over right against Jericho. And the priests that bare the ark of the covenant of the Lord stood firm on dry ground in the midst of Jordan, and all the Israelites passed over on dry ground, until all the people were passed clean over Jordan" (Joshua 3:16, 17).

They were out and they were in!

Joshua commanded twelve men, one out of every tribe, each to bring a stone from out of the midst of Jordan, from the place where the priests' feet had stood firm, and these he pitched in Gilgal, where Israel camped on their first day in the land. "And he spake unto the children of Israel, saying, When your children shall ask their fathers in time to come, saying, What mean these stones? Then ye shall let your children know, saying, Israel came over this Jordan on dry land" (Joshua 4:21, 22).

These stones were to remind the children of Israel of the principle to which they had returned, for as God had dried up the waters of the Red Sea, so God had dried up the waters of Jordan. "That all the people of the earth might know the hand of the Lord, that it is mighty" (Joshua 4:24).

How did they get through the Red Sea?

They put their feet in the water and stood still. Why? God told them to! What happened? God divided the waters and they passed through on dry ground. Why? God said they would!

How did they get through Jordan?

They put their feet in the waters of Jordan and stood still. Why? God told them to! What happened? God divided the waters and they went through on dry land. Why? God said they would!

How much more difficult then was it to get in than to get out? No more difficult! It was as easy to get in as it was to get out. And how long did it take them to discover this?

Forty years!

"As ye have received Christ Jesus the Lord, so walk ye in him" (Colossians 2:6).

How are you to walk in Jesus Christ? As you received Him. How did you receive Him? By faith. Was that very difficult?

How then are you to walk in Him? By faith! Will that be any more difficult?

As you have learned to thank Him for His death, so you thank Him for His life, humbly assuming that He lives in you, as you have already humbly assumed that He died for you. Is that not simple? And how long has it taken you to find this out?

Remember, He does not give you strength — He *is* your strength! He does not give you victory — He *is* your victory! He cannot be your *life* without being *all you need,* for "in him dwells all the fulness of the Godhead bodily, and you are complete in him" (Colossians 2:9).

Then count upon the fact — and stop asking for what you have!

"And the children of Israel encamped in Gilgal, and kept the passover on the fourteenth day of the month at even in the plains of Jericho. And they did eat of the old corn of the land on the morrow after the passover, unleavened cakes, and parched corn in the selfsame day" (Joshua 5:10, 11).

And so for the first time in forty years, they had legitimate grounds to celebrate the "day to be remembered in a land to be possessed," for that day, God had "rolled away the reproach of Egypt from off them."

For the first time the people began to enjoy that for which they had been redeemed, and their salvation made sense.

"And it came to pass, when Joshua was by Jericho, that he lifted up his eyes and looked, and, behold, there stood a man over against him with his sword drawn in his hand: and Joshua went unto him, and said unto him, Art thou for us, or for our adversaries?" (Joshua 5:13).

Joshua went out to make a reconnaissance of the walled city of Jericho and to draw up plans for tackling the first major task that confronted him, but as he did so he became strangely aware of the presence of a Man — a Man with His sword drawn in His hand — and in so many words, he said to Him, "Whose side are you on? Are you on our side or are you on their side?"

"And He said, Nay; but as captain of the host of the Lord am I now come."

The Man with the sword in His hand said, in effect, "I

am neither on your side nor am I on their side. I have come as
Captain of the host of the Lord. I have not come to take sides
— I have come to take over!"

In the land, you do not make your plans, hoping that
God will be on your side! Jericho is no longer *your* problem!
It is God's problem, and you come under the supreme jurisdic-
tion of the Man with the sword in His hand.

"And Joshua fell on his face to the earth, and did worship,
and said unto him, What saith my lord unto his servant?
And the captain of the Lord's host said unto Joshua, Loose
thy shoe from off thy foot; for the place whereon thou
standest is holy. And Joshua did so" (Joshua 5:14, 15).

He knew that he was in the presence of God, the God
of the burning bush. There had been no change of principle,
for God does not change. It was simply that Joshua had to relearn what Moses forgot.

God does not take sides — He only takes over!
Including your Jericho!
Are you prepared for this?

Victory and Vocation

12

Victory and Vocation

JESUS CHRIST HIMSELF IS THE FINAL EXEGESIS OF ALL TRUTH.
He is all that we need to know about God, and He is all that we
need to know about man, and if "to live in the land" is to enjoy
that quality of life which is made possible only by virtue of
allowing Him to live His life in us, we could not do better than
to conclude our studies in this book by turning our eyes again
upon Him, whose perfect humanity is matched only by His
perfect deity.

> Jesus knowing that the Father had given all things into his hands, and
> that he was come from God, and went to God; he riseth from supper,
> and laid aside his garments; and took a towel, and girded himself. After that
> he poureth water into a basin, and began to wash the disciples' feet, and
> to wipe them with the towel wherewith he was girded (John 13:3-5).

The Lord Jesus knew that the Father had given all
things into His hands — that as a Man, all the illimitable resources of deity had been vested in His person. That is the first
thing I would like you to notice, for although He was in the
beginning with God, and was God, and *is* God — and although
as the Creative Word, all things were made by Him — when
He came to this earth, in the very fullest sense of the term, He
became Man; but He became Man as God intended man to be,
and behaved as God intended man to behave, walking day by
day in that relationship to the Father which God had always
intended should exist between man and Himself.

> Who, although being essentially one with God *and* in the form of God
> (possessing the fulness of the attributes which make God God), did not
> think this equality with God was a thing to be eagerly grasped or
> retained; but stripped Himself (of all privileges and rightful dignity)
> so as to assume the guise of a servant (slave), in that He became like men
> *and* was born a human being. And after He had appeared in human form
> He abased *and* humbled Himself (still further) and carried His
> obedience to the extreme of death, even the death of [the] cross!
> (Philippians 2:6-8 *Amplified New Testament*).

141

We shall enlarge upon this as we proceed, but I mention it in particular now, that we may recognize the fact that in all His activities, in all His reactions, in every step He took and in every word He said, in every decision He made, He did so *as man*, even though He was God. He knew that in His perfection *as man*, the Father had vested in Him all that God intended to vest in man — all things! In other words, man in perfection has an unlimited call upon the inexhaustible supplies of deity.

To put it another way, all the inexhaustible supplies of God are *available* to the man who is *available* to all the in-inexhaustible supplies of God; and Jesus Christ was that Man! He was Man in perfection — totally, unrelentingly, unquestioningly available — and that is why there was available to Him all that to which He was available — all things! Now that is a principle to which we shall need to return on many occasions.

A second thing is this: He knew that He was come from God—that is to say, His divine origin; and He knew that He went to God — that is to say, His divine destination. He came from God and He was going to God. This is reiterated in John 16:27 — "The Father himself loveth you, because ye have loved me, and have believed that I came out from God. I came forth from the Father, and am come into the world: again, I leave the world, and go to the Father." *From* the Father *to* the Father, and in between 33 years on earth *in* the world; a parenthesis in time, as it were, with eternity on one side and eternity on the other, and a short limited time space — 33 years — on earth. He was in the beginning with God in the past — *of* the Father. He was to be eternally with God in the future — *to* the Father. But in the meantime for 33 years He must play the role of Man in perfection, and as such He knew that the Father had given all things into His hands — that He had come from God and was going to God!

One might imagine that at this stage we are poised upon the threshold of some sensational event or some sensational utterance; but instead it comes almost as an anti-climax to read that He rose from supper, laid aside His garments, took a towel, girded Himself, poured water into a basin, and washed His disciples' feet. With all the illimitable resources of deity —

of divine origin and divine destination — He washed His disciples' feet, something which was too lowly even for His own disciples, who felt themselves above such condescension.

Did He need all the illimitable resources of deity to wash His disciples' feet? *God* on His knees!

The Lord Jesus Christ was demonstrating a principle, that it is not the *nature* of what you are doing that determines its spirituality, but the *origin* of what you are doing. Not its nature, but its origin!

There was never a moment in the life of the Lord Jesus that was without divine significance, because there was never anything He did, never anything He said, never any step He took, which did not spring from a divine origin — nothing that was not the activity of the Father in and through the Son. Thirty-three years of availability to the Father, that the Father in and through Him might implement the program that had been established and agreed on between the Father and the Son before ever the world was.

Why did the Father give all things into His hands? Because Jesus Christ was completely Man. And He was completely Man because He was completely available! For the first time since Adam fell into sin, there was on earth a Man as God intended man to be!

Which of His activities were the more spiritual, the Sermon on the Mount, the raising of Lazarus from the dead, or the washing of His disciples' feet? The answer, of course, is that no one activity was more spiritual than another, for *all* had their origin in the Father, who acted through the Son. "I do always those things that please Him " (John 8:29). Spirituality in man is his availability to God for His divine action, and the *form* of this activity is irrelevant. If it pleases you, always and only, to do what pleases God — you can do as you please!

Let us consider two passages in the epistle to the Hebrews, which at first sight appear a little strange. Hebrews 2:9, 10 — "But we see Jesus, who was made a little lower than the angels for the suffering of death, crowned with glory and honour; that he by the grace of God should taste death for every man. For it became him, for whom are all things, and by whom are all things, in bringing many sons unto glory, to make the captain of their salvation perfect through sufferings." It was necessary for God the Father to make Him, God the Son, perfect through suffering.

Bearing that in mind, we now turn to Hebrews 5:8, 9, where it says, "Though he were a Son, yet learned he obedience by the things which he suffered; and being made perfect, he became the author of eternal salvation unto all them that obey him." In the second chapter it says that it was necessary for the Father to make Him perfect; in the fifth chapter it says that "being made perfect" He "became the author of eternal salvation." In other words, His "becoming" the author of our eternal salvation appears to have been dependent upon the successful conclusion of a process whereby He was "made" perfect.

He was "made perfect" in order to "become." Does that strike you as being a little bit strange? Was the Lord Jesus *not* perfect, that He needed to be made perfect? Was there, after all, in the Lord Jesus some blemish that needed to be rectified, some imperfection that had to be remedied, that He might "become the author of eternal salvation unto all them that obey Him"?

Here another principle is involved. The perfection of the Lord Jesus Christ was two-fold. The Bible leaves us in absolutely no doubt about the absolute perfection of His person. We are told that "God made him to be sin for us, who knew no sin; that we might be made the righteousness of God in him" (II Corinthians 5:21). We are told that when the Father looked down from heaven before the beginning of Christ's public ministry, in reviewing as it were the first thirty years that Christ had lived as Man on earth — as a little child, as a son, as an apprentice, as a craftsman, as a neighbor, as a citizen — the Father said, "This is my beloved Son, in whom (*in all these areas of human relationship*) I am well pleased" (Matthew 3:17).

Perfect! Perfect in person; but although He was perfect in person, He had to be made perfect in *vocation* — by the process of obedience through time, because as Man, perfect in person, He could only be perfect in vocation by the fulfillment of that purpose for which He had been incarnate, in an attitude of total dependence *upon* the Father expressed in total obedience *to* the Father. Being perfect in His person, he was "made perfect" in His vocation.

Was He perfect in vocation — in that purpose for which He was incarnate and came into this world — as a baby at Bethlehem? Had He been able to speak as a baby, could He then have said, "It is finished!"? As a boy of twelve when His mother found Him in the Temple, and He said to her, "Wist ye not that I must be about my Father's business?" — was He perfect in vocation? When He preached the Sermon on the Mount, or when He raised Lazarus from the dead, or even when He washed His disciples' feet — was He perfect in vocation? When He was in the Garden of Gethsemane, sweating as it were great drops of blood — was He perfect in vocation?

It was no idle boast when He spoke to Peter in the presence of Judas and of those who arrested Him, and said, "Thinkest thou that I cannot now pray to my Father, and he shall presently give me more than twelve legions of angels?" — but had He spoken that word, and had the Father sent twelve legions of angels, and had He by-passed the cross — would He have been perfect in the vocation for which He was incarnate? No indeed, and you and I would today be of all men most miserable, for there would not have been established any ground for redemption that could have satisfied the eternal, unrelenting, and absolute demands of God's holiness — but we are told that He set His face like a flint, He turned neither to the right hand nor to the left — He was "obedient unto death, even the death of the cross."

He was completely submissive to that purpose to which the Father was committed in Him, and as He hung upon the cross, the heavens were darkened as though in anguish for the Son of God for the space of three hours, and just before He bowed His head and died He was able to cry (and know that it was true) with a voice that reverberated in victory across the city of Jerusalem — "It is finished!" In that moment of time He was "made perfect" in His *vocation* as He had always been perfect in His *person,* and He "became the author of eternal salvation to them that obey him." That was the nature of *His* victory, and that is the nature of *all* Christian victory! The positive fulfillment of the divine end through a MAN, *wholly* available to GOD!

The Lord Jesus did not live a victorious life just because He did not commit sin in the negative sense; because He did not tell lies, because He was not dishonest; because He never committed adultery, and was never envious — that was not the nature of His victory. If that had been the nature of His victory and that the criterion of His righteousness, He could have stayed in heaven and been all that! The nature of His victory was that as Man He positively implemented that purpose for which He was incarnate; that apart from not doing the things that were *wrong*, He positively *accomplished* all that was *right;* that His absolute availability to the Father for every moment of 33 years enabled the Father in His deity to do in and through the Son in His humanity all that had been agreed on between the Father and the Son before ever the world was.

A sense of vocation declares, ". . . the things concerning me have an end!" (Luke 22:37), and the language of victory cries, "It is finished!" (John 19:30).

I want you to notice *how* Jesus Christ made Himself available to the Father. Hebrews 10:5-7 in the *Amplified New Testament* reads, "Hence, when He (Christ) entered into the world, He said, Sacrifices and offerings You have not desired, but instead You have made ready a body for Me [to offer]; in burnt offerings and sin offerings You have taken no delight. Then I said, Lo, here I am, come to do Your will, O God: [to fulfill] what is written of Me in the volume of the Book." Even as the whole redemptive purpose had been foreshadowed by the prophets to the fathers and recorded under the inspiration of the Holy Spirit "in the volume of the Book" — the written Word of the Old Testament scriptures — so now the Lord Jesus as the Living Word says in effect to the Father, "The body that You have prepared for Me, I now present to You, that all that has been written of Me in the volume of the Book may now find its complete consummation in My person."

By the offering of His body we must understand that this involved the offering of His total being as Man — body, soul, and spirit—in unreserved yielding of His human personality to the Father.

By what means, however, did the Lord Jesus Christ present His body to the Father, that during those 33 years the Father in and through the Son might implement all that had been written in the volume of the Book?

The answer to this question is found in Hebrews 9:14—"How much more shall the blood of Christ, who through the eternal Spirit offered himself without spot to God, purge your conscience from dead works to serve the living God?" The Son, as Man, gave Himself to the Father, as God, through the eternal Spirit, and the Father, as God, gave Himself to the Son, as Man, through the eternal Spirit—and through the eternal Spirit He walked, He moved and had His being. Every step He took, every word He spoke, everything He did, all that He was, was an expression of the Father as God, in the Son as Man, through the eternal Spirit.

To complete the picture, the Lord Jesus summarized this in John 14:10—"Believest thou not that I am in the Father, and the Father in me? the words that I speak unto you I speak not of myself: but the Father that dwelleth in me, he doeth the works." In other words, "I have presented My body to the Father who indwells Me, that He may do His works in my body; and My Father does His works through His Spirit by whom He indwells Me, and through whom I have offered Myself without spot, faultlessly, to my Father." So we understand that the whole activity of the Lord Jesus on earth as Man was the Father's activity in the Son, through the eternal Spirit through whom His body was presented to the Father.

Of the Father—through the Father—to the Father! That was the life of Jesus Christ on earth, from Bethlehem to the Mount of Olives. As MAN it was the office of the Son to *be,*—as GOD it was the office of the Father to *do!* Of His relationship to the Father the Son would say, "I am—He does! What I do, My Father does! What I say, My Father says! What I am, My Father is!"

"Jesus saith unto him, Have I been so long time with you, and yet hast thou not known me, Philip? he that hath seen me hath seen the Father; and how sayest thou then, Shew us the Father?" (John 14:9).

Now what does the Bible say regarding your relationship to the Lord Jesus? The Bible declares again and again from the lips of the Lord Jesus that your relationship to Him now must be what His relationship to the Father was then; that *as* the Father sent Him, *so* He sends you. "Just as the living Father sent Me, and I live by (through, because of) the Father, even so whoever continues to feed on Me — who takes Me for his food *and* is nourished by Me — shall [in his turn] live through *and* because of Me" (John 6:57 *Amplified New Testament*). So whatever you may discover to be the basis of the life of Christ, in His relationship to the Father, inevitably this must be the basis of your life in relationship to Him. That should not surprise you, indeed, if it is not so, it should shock you!

Next let us consider Romans 11:36 — "For of him, and through him, and to him, are all things: to whom be glory for ever. Amen." Of Him, through Him, and to Him! But that is precisely the relationship that existed between the Son as Man and the Father as God — of the Father, through the Father, and to the Father!

May I ask you a question? Do you have eternal life? You say, "Yes, thank God, I do!" Well, that is fine — but what *is* eternal life? Did you ever give yourself a satisfactory answer to that question?

What is eternal life? Is it a place that you are going to when you are dead? Is it a peculiar feeling inside? If you were to ask a normal congregation, or any sort of Bible class or Sunday school in an evangelical church to define eternal life, you would be amazed at the strange answers you would get!

What is eternal life? When does it begin? I noticed just the other day, in a hospital chapel where I was speaking, a tablet on the wall in memory of one of the previous chaplains, and in giving the date of his death it said, "He entered into eternal life." Is that true if he was a Christian? Is it right to imply, as did that tablet on the wall, that eternal life begins when a man is physically dead? No, indeed!

"And this is the record, that God hath given to us eternal life, and this life is in his Son. He that hath the Son hath life; and he that hath not the Son of God hath not life" (I John 5:11, 12).

Jesus Christ and eternal life are synonymous terms, and eternal life is none other than Jesus Christ Himself, of whom it is written in John 1:4 — "In him was life; and this life was the light of men." If you have eternal life at all, it simply means that you have the Son, Jesus Christ — NOW! Jesus said, "I *am* the Way, I *am* the Truth, I *am* the Life" (John 14:6).

Eternal life is not a peculiar feeling inside! It is not your ultimate destination, to which you will go when you are dead. If you are born again, eternal life is that quality of life that you possess right now, at this very moment, in your own physical body, with your own two feet on the ground, and in the world TODAY! And where does this life come from? Of Him! He *is* that Life!

When was your Bethlehem? In the day that Jesus Christ was formed in you! (Galatians 4:19). When He came to take up residence and inhabit your redeemed humanity as God by His gracious presence, through the eternal Spirit, so that your body became "the temple of the living God," and you were added to that body corporate called the Church, which Paul writing to the Ephesians describes as "a habitation of God through the Spirit" (Ephesians 2:22). So if you have eternal life, it means that you have *Somebody,* Jesus Christ, and the life that you possess is *of* Him.

Where is that life going to? If you were to die physically tonight, what would happen? The Bible says that you would be "absent from the body" and "present with the Lord" (II Corinthians 5:8). You would go *to* Him, whose resurrection life you now enjoy, imparted to you by His indwelling Holy Spirit.

If the Lord Jesus were to come again today, as well He may, you would not "precede them which are asleep" in Jesus but you would be "caught up together with them in the clouds to meet the Lord in the air"; and in this case also, you would go "to Him," whose resurrection life you now enjoy. So whether you sleep in Jesus, or are alive and remain at His coming, that eternal life which you now have is both of Him and to Him.

What is there in between? Between *your* Bethlehem, and *your* Mount of Olives? Thirty-three years? It could be! Or three years, or fifty, or six weeks. However, for whatever period of time you remain physically alive on earth, indwelt by Jesus Christ through His eternal Spirit — for many years or few — this is *your vocation!* That purpose for which as *man* you live on earth — that Christ might have His inheritance now, in you, on the way to heaven. Your humanity as unreservedly available to Him, as His humanity was once unreservedly available to the Father.

Romans 12:1 draws the logical conclusion from the argument of the last verse of chapter 11 — "I beseech you therefore, brethren, by the mercies of God, that ye present your bodies a living sacrifice" — just as He did to the Father, you do now to the Son — "holy, acceptable unto God, which is your reasonable service. And be not conformed to this world" — do not ape its methods, its techniques, its ways, or its spirit — "but be ye transformed by the renewing of your mind, that ye may prove what is that good, and acceptable, and perfect, will of God." As the "good, acceptable, and perfect will of God" was implemented by the Son through dependence on the Father, so that "good, acceptable, and perfect will of God" may be implemented by you through dependence on the Son.

This divine vocation into which you have been redeemed, as "His workmanship, created in Christ Jesus unto good works which God hath before ordained that you should walk in them" (Ephesians 2:10) can only be fulfilled in the energy and power of the One who indwells you now by His Spirit, as He walked once only in the energy and power of the Father who indwelt Him through the Spirit. Of Himself He said, "I can of mine own self do nothing" (John 5:19), and of you He says, in John 15:5, "Without me *you* can do nothing."

How much can you do without Him? Nothing! So what is everything you do without Him? Nothing!

It is amazing how busy you can be doing nothing! Did you ever find that out? "The flesh" — everything that you do apart from Him — "profiteth nothing" (John 6:63), and there is always the awful possibility, if you do not discover this principle, that you may spend a lifetime in the service of Jesus Christ *doing nothing!* You would not be the first, and you would not be the last — but that, above everything else, we must seek to avoid!

So you discover that the life which you possess as a born-again Christian is *of* Him, and it is *to* Him, and every moment that you are here on earth it must be *through* Him — of Him, through Him, to Him, *all* things! "I beseech you therefore, brethren, by the mercies of God, that ye present your bodies a living sacrifice" (Romans 12:1).

The Lord Jesus Christ claims the use of *your* body, *your* whole being, *your* complete personality, so that as you give yourself to Him through the eternal Spirit, He may give Himself to you through the eternal Spirit, that all your activity as a human being on earth may be His activity in and through you; that every step *you* take, every word *you* speak, everything *you* do, everything *you* are, may be an expression of the Son of God, in you as man.

If it is *of Him* and *through Him* and *to Him,* where do *you* come in? You do not! That is just where you go out! That is what Paul meant when he said, "For me to live is *Christ*" (Philippians 1:21). The only Person whom God credits with the right to live in you is Jesus Christ; so reckon yourself to be dead to all that you are *apart* from what He is, and alive unto God only in all that you are *because* of what He is (Romans 6:11).

When the world looked at Jesus Christ, they saw God! They heard Him speak and they saw Him act. And Jesus said, "As my Father hath sent me, even so send I you" (John 20:21). The world again will hear God speak and see God act!

It is for you to BE — it is for Him to DO! Restfully available to the Saving Life of Christ, enjoying "the richest measure of the divine Presence, a body wholly filled and flooded with God Himself," instantly obedient to the heavenly impulse — this is your vocation, and this is your victory!

"I assure you, most solemnly I tell you, if anyone steadfastly believes in Me, he will himself be able to do the things that I do; and he will do even greater things than these, because I go to the Father. And I will do — I Myself will grant — whatever you may ask in My name [presenting all I AM] so that the Father may be glorified *and* extolled in [through] the Son" (John 14:12, 13 (*Amplified New Testament*).